ELY TO KINGS LYNN

Richard Adderson and
Graham Kenworthy

Series editor Vic Mitchell

Cover picture: Two smartly turned out "Claud Hamilton" class 4-4-0s bask in the sunshine shortly before the outbreak of World War II. No 8836 emits a pall of black smoke as it awaits departure time, whilst the driver of no 8790 has time to chat to a colleague as the last parcels are loaded into the clerestory-roofed van at the front of his train. (Stations UK)

First published October 2000
Reprinted January 2002

ISBN 1 901706 53 2

Design David Pede

Published by
Middleton Press
Easebourne Lane
Midhurst, West Sussex
GU29 9AZ
Tel: 01730 813169
Fax: 01730 812601

Printed & bound by Biddles Ltd,
Guildford and King's Lynn

CONTENTS

INDEX

I. Railways of the area in 1922. (R.Joby)

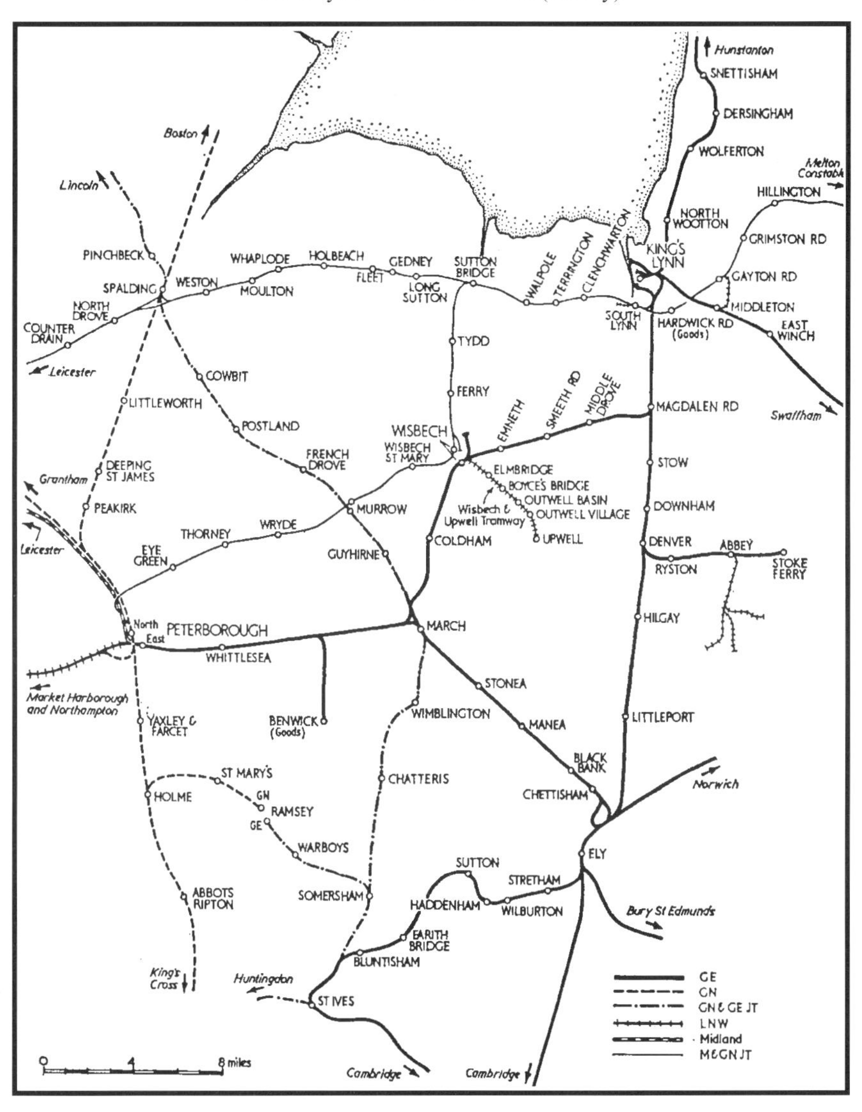

GEOGRAPHICAL SETTING

The Ely to Kings Lynn route is a fenland railway in every sense. The landscape is almost entirely flat and criss-crossed by numerous watercourses while the main river artery, the Great Ouse, and its flood relief channel are never more than a mile or so away from the line for the whole distance. As a consequence there are no gradients of note and much of the track is straight.

Ely station is just under 70½ miles from Liverpool Street and at this point, the Ouse is on the east of the line, a matter of a few yards from the station level crossing. Within a ½ mile the line crosses and recrosses the river, which then remains to the east and parallels the route for the next 12 miles. 1½ miles north of the station, at Ely North Junction, the Peterborough and Norwich routes diverge to west and east respectively, while that to Kings Lynn heads virtually due north towards the Fens of West Norfolk, crossing the county border out of Cambridgeshire about three miles north of Littleport.

A brief climb starts about one mile north of Hilgay in order to cross the Great Ouse, its tributary, the Wissey, and a Cut-off Channel; this presents the only obvious gradient on the whole section. Within a very short distance the line drops back to the level of the Fen at Denver, former junction for the Stoke Ferry branch. It is from this point onwards to Kings Lynn that the only semblance of higher ground appears in the landscape as a low scarp appears to the east, backed by the uplands of Central Norfolk. For the remaining 12 miles the railway runs virtually dead level and to the east of the Great Ouse, and its parallel Flood Relief Channel, constructed following the disastrous floods of 1947 and 1953.

The line skirts the eastern edge of Kings Lynn before curving westwards through 90° and terminating 96¾ miles from Liverpool Street.

Stoke Ferry Branch.

From the north facing junction at Denver, the Stoke Ferry branch swung sharply through a right angle and headed almost due east, skirting the southern edge of the low scarp mentioned above. After an initial minor climb and descent in the first two miles the line followed the northern edge of the fen on shallow gradients before terminating adjacent to the main road from Downham Market to Thetford.

Maps used in this volume are to a scale of 25 ins to 1 mile unless otherwise stated.

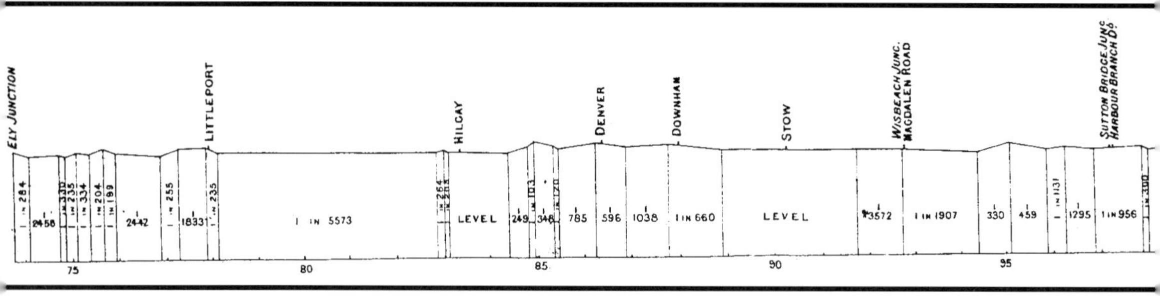

II. Gradient diagram of the line. The mileposts shown are as they existed when the diagram was produced in the 1870s, with the mileage from Bishopsgate (London) via Stratford.. In the 1930s, a remeasurement of the route from Liverpool Street via Hackney Downs reduced the official distance to Kings Lynn by just under two miles.

HISTORICAL BACKGROUND

Although the town of Kings Lynn had been officially known as such since its renaming from Bishops Lynn in 1537, railways, both proposed and actual, knew it simply as "Lynn"; this situation did not change until 1911 when the GER adopted the full title officially. Prior to the coming of the Railway Age to the Eastern Counties, Lynn was a wealthy port, lying, as it did, at the mouth of the Great Ouse which, with its navigable tributaries, served parts of no less than seven counties. However, the complacency of the businessmen of the town and their reluctance to adapt to the new opportunities offered by the railways was almost its economic downfall. William Armes, a prominent commentator on the 19th century development of Kings Lynn, stated that "On the introduction of the new system of railways and free trade, the corn merchants of Lynn became naturally alarmed. They said their occupation was gone, and they, in some cases, evidenced their sincerity by entirely abandoning their premises and retiring from the conflict. The whole aspect along the river was changed- TO BE LET was posted upon several extensive warehouses which, but a very short time previously, many enterprising men would have been anxious to hire".

That this state of affairs was averted is due to the energies of a Lynn solicitor, J.C.Williams, who was, however, more intent on making a personal fortune than fostering the interests of the town. He was responsible for promoting (among others) the Act for the Lynn & Ely which passed through Parliament in the Summer of 1845. The Act also provided for the construction of a branch to the Harbour at Lynn and a branch from Watlington to Wisbech. Unfortunately, authority coincided with the height of the Railway Mania, and all qualified surveyors and engineers were busy preparing schemes for the next Parliamentary session. This led to the non-availability of sufficient surveyors and engineers to oversee site works until early in 1846, when the contract for the first part of the line from Lynn to Denver, together with the Harbour Branch, was let. Due to the nature of the terrain, progress was rapid and, following inspection by the Board of Trade's Inspecting Officer, passenger services started on 27th October 1846. In addition to the terminus at Lynn, stations were provided at St.Germans, Watlington, Holme (almost exactly halfway between Watlington and Stow, from early 1847), Stow, Downham and Denver. The last named was opened, with minimal facilities, in early 1847 as Denver Road Gate, when three trains were extended from Downham on Lynn market days, Tuesdays and Saturdays.

The contract for the section southwards from Denver to Ely was let shortly after the first, in the Summer of 1846. However, this portion proved more difficult from an engineering point of view, particularly where a lengthy embankment had to be raised between Denver and Hilgay in order to carry the railway over the Rivers Ouse and Wissey at the height laid down in the Act. As a consequence, the line was not opened to public services until 25th October 1847, a few days after the Board of Trade inspection. Three intermediate stations were provided on this section, at Ouze (sic) Bridge, Hilgay Fen and Littleport, trains using the Eastern Counties Railway station at Ely.

Both sections were opened as single lines with passing loops at most of the stations. Provision was made for the line to be doubled, and the first part of the route to be so treated, by August 1847, was from Lynn to Watlington, the section which also carried traffic between Lynn and Wisbech. Hilgay Fen to Downham followed in September 1848.

Meanwhile, by an Act of 1847, the Lynn & Ely had been formally amalgamated with the Lynn & Dereham and the Ely & Huntingdon to form the East Anglian Railways Company, a course of action which had been planned since 1845. For a number of reasons, the company had been in financial trouble almost from the outset and plans to double the remainder of the line between Ely and Lynn were postponed indefinitely when the Official Receiver was called in June 1850. Two years later the Eastern Counties Railway took over the working of the EAR, although the latter remained a independent company until both (along with a number of other companies) were included in the arrangements which led to the formation of the Great Eastern Railway in 1862.

The remaining sections of single line, between Ely North Junction and Hilgay Fen, and between Downham and Watlington (renamed Magdalen Road in 1875) were doubled between 1881 and 1884 in conjunction with the modernisation of the signalling on the whole route. It was broadly in this form that the line survived the absorption of the GER into the London & North Eastern Railway in 1923 and the formation of British Railways (Eastern Region) in 1948.

There were various closures following the 1963 Beeching Report, particularly that of the line from Magdalen Road to Wisbech, on 9th September 1968. Apart from these, the main route remained largely intact until the early 1980s.

Almost exactly a century on from the events mentioned in the paragraph above, the process was reversed when singling of the line between Littleport and Downham took place on 17th June 1984, and from Magdalen Road to Kings Lynn Junction on 10th February 1985; on the latter section, there had been a three month period of temporary arrangements in connection with the abolition of Harbour Junction Signal Box. Multiple aspect signalling and level crossing modernisation was introduced at the same time.

The line became a northern outpost of Network SouthEast (NSE) on 10th June 1986.

The 1984/5 modernisation was followed, much to the surprise of many, by electrification in 1992, the full electric service starting on 24th August of that year. Following Privatisation on 5th January 1997 passenger services have been operated by West Anglia Great Northern, part of the Prism Group.

Stoke Ferry Branch.

Some twenty-odd years into the local "Railway Age" Stoke Ferry, the highest navigable point on the River Wissey and the centre for a number of small farming communities, was still trading by water or by inadequate local roads to either Denver or Downham. Closure of Denver station to passengers in 1870 and the failure of a number of schemes which would have added Stoke Ferry to the railway map, prompted local landowners to join forces to lobby the GER for a line to connect the area to the main line. The result was the formation of a separate company, the Downham and Stoke Ferry (despite the proposed junction being at Denver), which by an Act of 1879 would finance and build the railway to GER standards; on completion, the GER would work and staff the line in return for 50% of the receipts, while guaranteeing fixed dividends to the D&SFR shareholders. After largely trouble-free construction work and the usual inspection by the Board of Trade Inspector, the line opened on 1st August 1882.

Traffic never reached expectations and in 1895, the GER proposed the purchase of the D&SFR, the absorption finally being authorised in 1897. In anticipation of this event the GER introduced a number of modifications to the line, the most significant of which was the closure of the booking offices and introduction of conductor-guard working in March 1895. Freight and parcel traffic continued to provide a steady, if unspectacular, income.

The opening of the Wissington Light Railway by Mr A.J.Keeble in November 1905 revitalised the local economy and the Stoke Ferry branch. Branching off the line just east of Abbey station, the line headed southwards into a large area of fenland. Further areas were opened up by extensions built by a subsequent owner between 1925 and 1929. 1925 also saw the opening of the sugar beet processing factory about two miles south of Abbey.

The passenger service was withdrawn, following declining receipts, in September 1930, and an Order to convert the line to Light Railway status was made at the end of 1931. The branch saw a resurgence of traffic during World War II, mainly due to a government backed refurbishment of the Wissington Light Railway, a backing which continued because of post-war difficulties beyond the 1948 Nationalisation until 1957, when the line south of the sugar beet factory was closed.

Following the Beeching Report facilities were withdrawn from all stations, including Denver, between mid-1964 and mid-1966, leaving only movements to and from the sugar beet factory. Despite upgrading of both the branch and the Wissington line to cater for heavier axle loads, the declining traffic finally came to a halt at the end of the 1981/2 sugar beet season, known locally as the "campaign".

PASSENGER SERVICES

All examples quoted are from Winter period timetables and refer to trains which ran on most weekdays.

Early timetables showed a service of three daily passenger trains in each direction. That for October 1848 was typical, showing departures from Ely at 10.30 am, 2.30 pm and 8.35 pm, while trains left Lynn at 8.30 am, 11.50 am and 5.30 pm. All of these trains were shown to call at all stations. Services between Watlington and Lynn were supplemented by four trains each way to and from Wisbech; these also called intermediately at St. Germans.

By the January 1871 timetable, by which time Ouse Bridge, Denver, Holme and St.Germans had been closed, there were still only three daily trains in each direction between Ely and Lynn calling, apparently, at all remaining stations; however, a footnote added that, as far as Hilgay Fen and Stow were concerned, "The trains although noted in the tables to call, will not do so, except there are passengers to take up or set down." Watlington now only enjoyed three further services in each direction between Wisbech and Lynn.

The timetable in force from November 1899 to February 1900 reflected the gradual improvements which had taken place on the GER during the 1890s. There were now four "all stations" trains in the down direction, conditional stops having been eliminated. These were supplemented by a service leaving Ely at 4.35 pm, calling at Littleport and Downham only. Two further trains linked Ely with Lynn, but were routed via Wisbech, departing at 10.08 pm and 12.30 am; thus only Magdalen Road, of the intermediate stations, saw any benefit from these. In the up direction there was a total of seven trains, three of which called at all stations, a further two called at Downham and Littleport, the other two only troubling the staff at Downham. Ely could also be reached by two through trains via Wisbech, both making calls at Magdalen Road. This last station had also seen a slight increase in service of other trains from Wisbech, stops being made by five down and four up trains

In the Winter timetable for 1929/30 the four "all stations" down remained, while there were also three services designated "express passenger", one calling at Downham only, one at Littleport and Downham, and one at these last two plus Magdalen Road. The up trains were somewhat different, there being only six in total; there were four "all stations", one all stations except Hilgay but only one identified as an "express passenger" calling at Downham and Littleport. By this time Magdalen Road had achieved the dizzy heights of eight further daily services in each direction to and from Kings Lynn by virtue of trains using the Wisbech Branch.

Post-World War II services typified by the 1951/2 timetable indicate five down "all stations" trains and two others serving only Littleport and Downham. The latter included "The Fenman" which ran only on Mondays to Fridays, but there was an equivalent train on Saturdays running approximately ½ hour later. Up services were provided at an identical level. Magdalen Road's position at the junction of the Wisbech line continued to benefit the local travellers to Kings Lynn, but now only to the tune of six trains per day.

The Winter of 1958/9 was, to all intents and purposes, the start of the Diesel Age in East Anglia, and saw an almost complete transformation in service on the route. In order to make better use of stock, the decision was taken to withdraw most through services from Liverpool Street to Norwich via Cambridge and to divert them to Kings Lynn. This arrangement lasted for around thirty years and the 1969/70 timetable was typical of the period. Of the eight down and nine up trains between Ely and Kings Lynn, no less than twelve (six in each direction) were formed by through services to and from Liverpool Street, complete with catering facilities. All eight down trains called at all two remaining intermediate stations, while seven of the up services did likewise, the other two running non-stop.

From the completion of the electrification from Liverpool Street to Cambridge in 1987 until its extension to Kings Lynn in 1992, services to the West Norfolk capital suffered a period of what some saw as neglect. But the long awaited scheme was finally completed and saw a dramatic upturn in the line's fortunes resulting in a service level in 1999/2000 unimagined less than ten years earlier. The timetable for that Winter showed 18 up trains and 17 down between Ely and Kings Lynn. All of them called at all stations, and 34 of them provided a through service to and from London, but via the former Great Northern route to Kings Cross, rather than to the traditional terminus at Liverpool Street. (It is worth pointing out that on Mondays to Fridays at this time, there was a total of 44 trains, all but one of which were to or from London; of these, two up morning and three down evening commuter trains used Liverpool Street)

Stoke Ferry Branch.

As has been mentioned, the railway was actually called the Downham and Stoke Ferry, the service being provided between those points. The initial timetable consisted of six return trips, starting from Stoke Ferry at 7.58 am and finishing there at 8.10 pm; one up train, the 5.5 pm from Stoke Ferry was designated "mixed".

ELY, DOWNHAM, and KING'S LYNN

Miles		Week Days mrn	mrn	mrn	aft	E	S	aft	Suns mrn	aft
	4 London (L'pool St.) dep	5 45	8 20	1155	2 20	445	455	5Z49	8 20	220
	4 Cambridge ″	8 9	10 2	1 30	4 2	614	623	7Z25	10 2	4 2
—	Ely dep	8 37	1032	1 57	4 30	642	651	7 58	1032	430
5¼	Littleport	8 50	1043	2 8	4 41	653	7 2	8 9	1043	442
11	Hilgay	9 1	1053	2 18	4 51	..	..	8 19	1053	452
15¼	Downham	9 12	11 3	2 28	5 1	710	719	8 29	11 3	5 3
18¼	Stow Bardolph	9 17	11 8	2 33	5 6	..	..	8 34	11 8	5 8
20½	Magdalen Road	9 24	1114	2 39	5 12	..	..	8 40	1114	514
26½	King's Lynn arr	9 35	1124	2 49	5 24	727	736	8 50	1124	524
41½	41 Hunstanton arr	1025	12 8	3 40	6 9	8 8	817	9 33	12 8	6 8
53	42 Dereham ″	..	1 57	4 5	6 50	..	..	..	..	..
42	39 Wisbech ″	1014	2 49	4 53	6 13	..		10E58	..	..

	Week Days mrn	mrn	mrn	mrn	aft	aft	Suns. mrn	aft	aft
39 Wisbech dep	..	7 55	..	11 55	..	441	..	..	..
42 Dereham ″	..	8 24	..	11§32	1 0	416	..	..	..
41 Hunstanton ″	6 47	8 47	1043	aft	2 50	450	8 50	250	..
King's Lynn dep	7 31	9 32	1124	1 40	3 35	532	9 32	332	5 30
Magdalen Road	7 42	9 43	1135	1 51	3 46	543	9 43	343	5 41
Stow Bardolph	7 48	9 49	1141	1 57	3 52	549	9 49	349	5 47
Downham	7 55	9 56	1148	2 3	3 59	556	9 56	356	5 54
Hilgay	8 4	10 5	1157	2 12	4 8	6 5	10 5	4 5	6 3
Littleport	8 14	1015	12 7	2 22	4 18	615	1015	415	6 13
Ely arr	8 24	1025	1217	2 32	4 2[illegible]	625	1025	425	6 23
4 Cambridge arr	8 53	1058	1253	3 35	5 [illegible]	7 1	1058	456	6 48
4 London (L.St.) ″	1027	1240	2 34	6§16	6 [illegible]	848	1240	640	8 25

§ Except Saturdays. Third class only between Cambridge and London (L. St.). E or E Except Saturdays.
S Saturdays only. U Tuesdays only. Z Dep. London (L. St.) 5 52 and Cambridge 7 33 aft on Mons. and Fris.

January 1943

September 1951

ELY, DOWNHAM, and KING'S LYNN

Miles		Week Days a.m	a.m	a.m	a.m	a.m S	a.m	p.m	p.m	p.m	p.m	p.m EB	p.m S	p.m	p.m	p.m	p.m S	p.m H	Sundays a.m		p.m	p.m	p.m
	4 London (L'pool St.) dep	5 50	..	8 20	..	10 0	1150	..	12S27	2Y25	..	4 30	5 0	..	5F51	7 20	10 5	10g 5	8 20	..	2 25	6 0	8 10
	4 Cambridge ″	8 10	8 20	10 2	1020	1141	1p25	1d35	2 33	4 5	4d10	6 4	6 27	6d33	7F28	8 52	1225	12 15	10 4	..	4 15	7 32	9 40
—	Ely dep	8 37	8 55	1036	1050	1 5	1 58	2 15	3 22	4 40	4 50	6 28	6 56	6H50	8 8	9 22	1 0	2a15	10 45	..	4 45	8 6	10 9
5¼	Littleport	8 49	Via March	1047	Via March	1 16	2 9	Via March	Via March	4 51	Via March	6 39	7 7	Via March	8 19	9 33	1 11	Via March	10 56	..	4 56	8 17	10 20
11	Hilgay	8 59		1056		1 26	2 19			5 1		..	..		8 29	..	..		11 6	..	5 6	..	10‡29
15¼	Downham	9 8		11 5		1 35	2 29			5 11		6 56	7 24		8 39	9 49	1 27		11 16	..	5 16	8 34	10 39
18¼	Stow Bardolph	9 14		1110		1 40	2 34			5 16		..	..		8 44	..	..		11 21	..	5 21	..	10‡44
20½	Magdalen Road	9 21	10 14	1116	1218	1 48	2 40	3 39	4 49	5 22	6 27	Xx	..	8 30	8 50	..	..	..	11 27	..	5 27	..	10 50
26½	King's Lynn arr	9 32	10 25	1126	1229	2 1	2 50	3 50	4 59	5 34	6 38	7 14	7 41	8 40	9 0	10 7	1 43	3 35	11 38	..	5 37	8 51	11 0
41½	52 Hunstanton arr	10 13	..	12 9	1 55	..	3 37	..	..	6 16	..	7 55	8 23	..	9 44	..	..	..	12 20	..	6 20	9 30	..
53	54 Dereham ″	10 53		1N43	1 43	..	4 5	5T 4	..	6 41	..	..	9 50	9S50	..	..	..	..	..	..	..	..	..

THE FENMAN (p.m EB column)

Miles		Week Days a.m	a.m EB	a.m S	a.m	a.m	a.m	a.m	a.m	a.m.	p.m	p.m	p.m	p.m	p.m	p.m E	p.m S		Sundays a.m	p.m	p.m	p.m	p.m
	54 Dereham dep	..	..	..	..	6 55	8 12	..	..	11T 5	1 5	1 5	..	4K10	..	7 10	7 10	..	..	..	..	..	..
	52 Hunstanton ″	..	6 45	6 45	..	..	8 45	11 0	..	12p35	1S19	2 45	3 28	4 50	..	7 30	7 30	..	8 47	2 50	4 45	5 45	..
—	King's Lynn dep	6 30	7 30	7 30	7 35	8 4	9 30	11 43	1148	1 18	2 15	3 30	4 18	5 32	5 38	10 30	10 40	..	9 30	3 32	5 25	6 22	8 41
6	Magdalen Road	6 41	..	..	7 46	8 15	9 41	..	1159	1 29	2 26	3 41	4 29	5 43	5 49	10 41	10 51	..	9 41	3 43	5 36	..	8 52
8¼	Stow Bardolph	Via March	..	..	7 52	Via March	9 47	..	Via March	1 35	Via March	3 47	Via March	5 49	Via March	Via March	10 57	..	9 47	3 49	5 42	..	8 58
10½	Downham		7 46	7 46	8 1		9 54	12 0		1 42		3 54		5 56			11 4	..	9 54	3 56	5 49	6 39	9 5
15¼	Hilgay		..	..	8 10		10 3	..		1 51		4 3		6 5			11 13	..	10 3	4 5	5 58	..	..
20¼	Littleport		..	..	8 21		10 13	12 14		2 1		4 13		6 15			11 23	..	10 13	4 15	6 8	..	9 22
26¼	Ely arr	8 0	8 9	8 9	8 30	10 1	10 23	12 24	1 30	2 11	4 6	4 23	6 15	6 28	7 51	11 48	11 33	..	10 24	4 27	6 18	7 4	9 32
41¼	4 Cambridge arr	..	8 31	8 31	9 0	10d41	10 57	12 56	..	2 40	4d18	4 58	6d52	6 58	8 23	12a51	12a10	..	11 0	5 3	6 46	7 41	10 5
97	4 London (L'pool St.) ″	..	10 3	10 3	10S34	..	12 37	2 33	..	5y 0	..	6J45	..	8 43	11 17	2a28	2a28	..	12p40	6 38	8 20	9 2	2a38

THE FENMAN (a.m EB and a.m S columns)

a a.m.
B Buffet Car between Liverpool Street and Hunstanton
B Passengers can arr. King's Cross 10 45 a.m. via Cambridge
d Via St. Ives
E or E Except Saturdays
F Dep. Liverpool St. 5 55 and Cambridge 7 42 p.m. on Fridays until 26th October, inclusive
g Passengers can dep. 10 30 p.m. via Ipswich and Haughley
H Except Saturday ngts and Sunday morns.
H Dep. 7 2 p.m. on Saturdays
J Arr. 6 42 p.m. on Saturdays
K Dep. 4 15 p.m. on Saturdays
N Arr. 12 37 p.m. on Saturdays

April 1910

DOWNHAM and STOKE FERRY.—Great Eastern.

Miles	Down.	Week Days. mrn		mrn	aft	aft	aft		aft	aft		aft	
	Downham dep.	8 44	Mons.	1025	1218	2 40	4 20	Tues.	6 t 0	6 49	Mons. and Fris.	7 40	Sats. only.
1¼	Denver	8 49		1030	1223	2 45	4 25		6 t 5	6 54		7 45	
3	Ryston	8 54		1040	1228	2 50	4 30		6t10	6 59		7 50	
5¼	Abbey ‡	9 1		1047	1235	2 57	4 37		6t17	7 6		7 57	
8¼	Stoke Ferry arr.	9 9		1055	1243	3 5	4 45		6t25	7 14		8 5	

Miles	Up.	Week Days. mrn		mrn	mrn	aft	aft	aft	
	Stoke Ferry dep.	8 10	Mons.	9 18	1117	1 50	5 15	6 55	Sats. only.
3¼	Abbey ‡	8 19		9 27	1126	1 59	5 24	7 4	
5¼	Ryston	8 26		9 34	1133	2 6	5 31	7 11	
7¼	Denver	8 31		9 39	1138	2 14	5 36	7 16	
8¼	Downham 301 arr.	8 35		9 43	1142	2 20	5 40	7 20	

t Except Mondays and Fridays. ‡ Station for West Dereham (1¼ miles).

This very soon fell to five return trips and by the October 1905 timetable had fallen further, to four, starting at 9.18 am from the terminus and finishing there at either 6.25 pm (on Tuesdays, Wednesdays, Thursdays and Saturdays) or 7.11 pm (on Mondays and Fridays).

The final timetable for the Summer of 1930 showed an identical level of service, but to a slightly different pattern, starting from Stoke Ferry at 8.25 am, the last train of the day arriving back at three different times, 6.22 pm on Wednesdays and Thursdays, 6.27 pm on Tuesdays and 6.37 pm on the remainder.

A rare luggage label which dates from around 1950.
It was coloured orange and blue.(R.Knight)

ACKNOWLEDGEMENTS

In addition to those acknowledged in the photographic credits, particularly the photographers, we are most grateful to the following people for their assistance in the compilation of this book; R.Barham, R.Baxter, D.Medlock (Campbells Grocery Products Ltd.), S.Taylor and M.Bignell (both of the Potter Group)

Readers of this book may be interested in the following societies:

Great Eastern Railway Society J.R.Tant Membership Secretary, 9 Clare Road, Leytonstone London E11 1JU;
M&GN Circle G.L.Kenworthy Membership Secretary, 16 Beverley Road, Brundall Norwich NR13 5QS.

1. Ely to Denver Junction

ELY

1. The photographer has taken advantage of a low Winter sun to illuminate the north-eastern approach to the station in 1911, but the glowing lamp in the foreground suggests that the favourable lighting conditions will be short lived. Beyond the muddy road, Ely North signalbox overlooks a complicated track layout, as the double track over the river bridge widens to three platform roads and a through line, and also gives access to the covered coal sidings to the left. In the siding on the right, two men and two horses are busily occupied shunting a horse-box and an ancient 4-wheel coach. The flooded fields on the far side of the railway show that the Great Ouse has overflowed its banks, and as we continue our journey, we shall see further evidence of the continual battle to drain this low-lying region. (National Railway Museum)

2. Class B12 4-6-0 no. 61575 departs northwards with the Kings Lynn portion of a train from Liverpool Street on 20th May 1957. The other section is already on its way to Norwich, behind the "Britannia" which had brought the combined train from London. (R.C.Riley)

3. A class 365 EMU heads north from the station on 11th March 2000. The signalling over a much simplified track layout is controlled from Cambridge, some 15 miles away, and the station nameboard publicises WAGN (West Anglia Great Northern) Railways, who have operated the Kings Lynn service since Privatisation. (R.J.Adderson)

NORTH OF ELY

4. With the cathedral looming above it, no. 47579 *James Nightall G.C.* crosses the river bridge as it leaves the station with a train for Kings Lynn on 30th August 1988. The cathedral dominates the area, and can be seen from several miles away on all the rail routes radiating from the city. (J.Cordle)

5. No. 47060 accelerates away from the junction towards the station with the daily Speedlink train from Whitemoor to Kings Lynn on a March day in 1991. After the loco has run round the train in the station, it will return to the junction where it will take the second left turn to continue its journey. Behind the train are the junction signal box, dating from 1926, and its down home signal gantry. (J.Cordle)

ELY NORTH JUNCTION

III. This map at a scale of 6 inches to 1 mile illustrates the complications of the track layout at this location with the divergence of the routes (from left to right) to March, Kings Lynn and Norwich, the connection to the sugar beet factory and the avoiding curve between the North and West Junctions; despite being identified here as Ely South Curve it was also known officially at various times in its history as Ely North Curve and Ely West Curve. The railway dominated settlement of Queen Adelaide is shown to good effect.

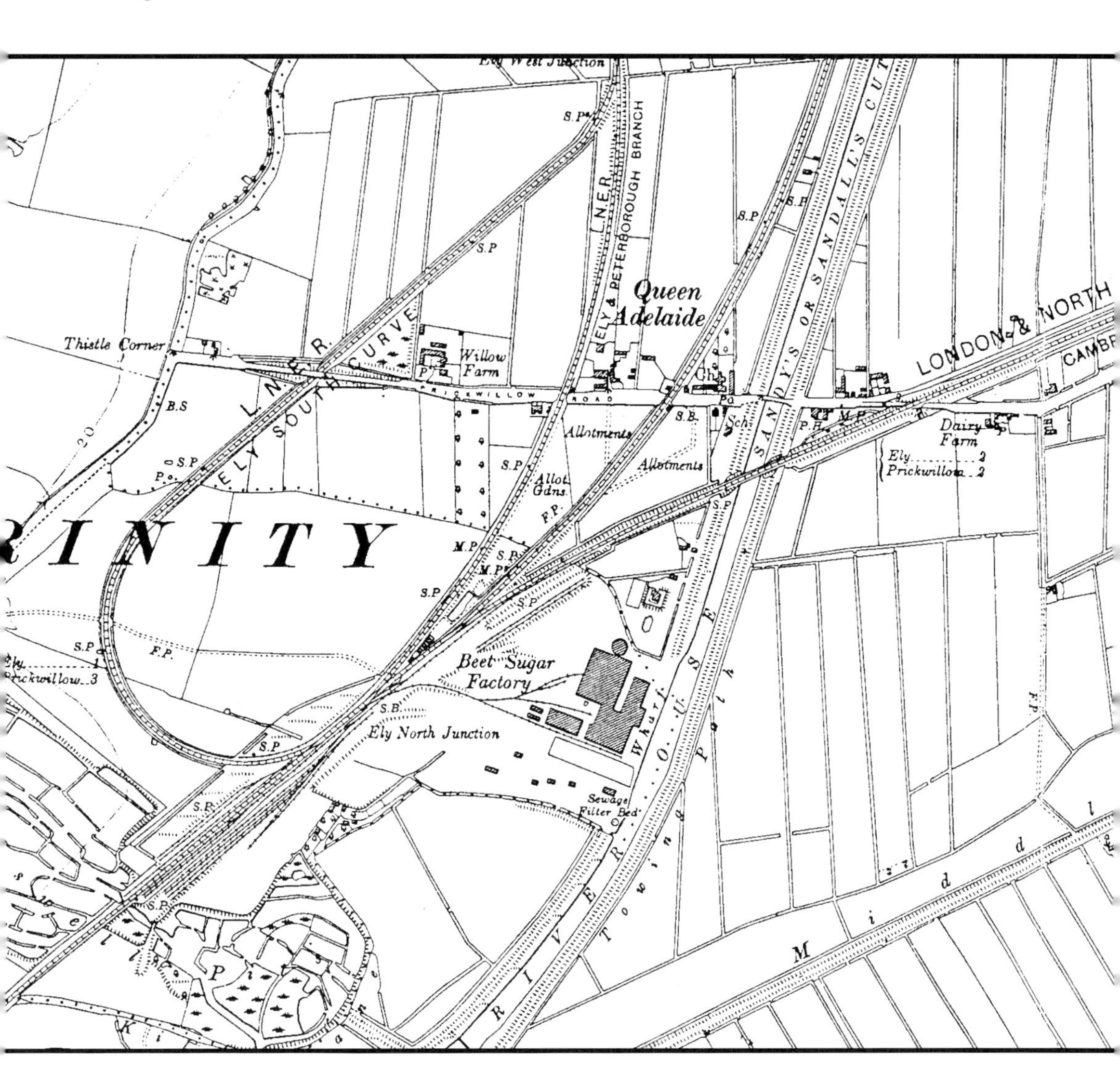

Other views of Ely and this junction can be found in **Branch Lines around March.**

6. At the junction, trains for Kings Lynn fork right and then left in quick succession. In this 1911 view the slightly awkward alignment of the Kings Lynn line diverges from the original route to Norwich by the signal. Nearer the cameraman, the line to March and Peterborough heads away to the left of a distinctive octagonal building, which dates back to the opening of the railway in 1845. (National Railway Museum)

→

7. The sugar beet factory started production in 1925 and was rail served from the beginning. A connection with the main line has just been installed, whilst lengths of the narrow gauge track used during the construction work litter the muddy site on 26th November 1924. Beyond the gate the old signal box, supported by massive timbers, is looking somewhat ramshackle, and it is no surprise that it was replaced within fifteen months. (Potter Group)

→

8. The contractors' locomotive, Manning Wardle 0-6-0ST *Sirdar*, busies itself during construction work on 12th December 1924. This engine had arrived on site earlier in the year, and obviously found the bracing fenland air to its taste, for it became the factory shunter after the work was completed, and survived in this role until 1950. (Potter Group)

9. Following the closure of the sugar beet factory in 1980, the site was taken over by the Potter Group as a rail connected distribution depot. No. 66136 sets back into the yard on 30th November 1999 with the daily train, which has run as a block load from Doncaster; within an hour or so it will be on its way back with the outward wagons. Behind the locomotive we can see the simplified junction layout, which dates from 1992. (R.J.Adderson)

10. Summing up the integration of road and rail at the site, a Potter Group lorry stands next to a Rolls Royce engined 0-6-0 diesel shunter, again on 30th November 1999. Rail traffic doubled from 200 wagons per month in 1981-1996 to 400 wagons per month between 1996 and 1999, and by the end of the century, the goods handled here included animal feed, South Wales coal, beetroot, aggregates, molasses, paper, chipboard, chalk powder and canned foods. (G.L.Kenworthy)

NORTH OF ELY NORTH JUNCTION

11. The road through this little settlement of Queen Adelaide crosses four railway lines in less than a mile, three of them on the level. In the centre of this picture, we have a rare glimpse of the signal box by the level crossing on the Kings Lynn line. Known officially, and less regally, as plain "Adelaide", it was abolished in 1929. (Cambridgeshire Collection, Cambridge Central Library)

12. Beyond Queen Adelaide the railway and the Great Ouse run dead straight and parallel in a northerly direction for some three miles. A 3-car class 101 DMU makes its way towards Ely across the lonely landscape just south of Littleport on 19th October 1991. At this time through services between London and Kings Lynn had been withdrawn owing to electrification work, and trains were running between Cambridge and Kings Lynn only. (R.J.Adderson)

LITTLEPORT

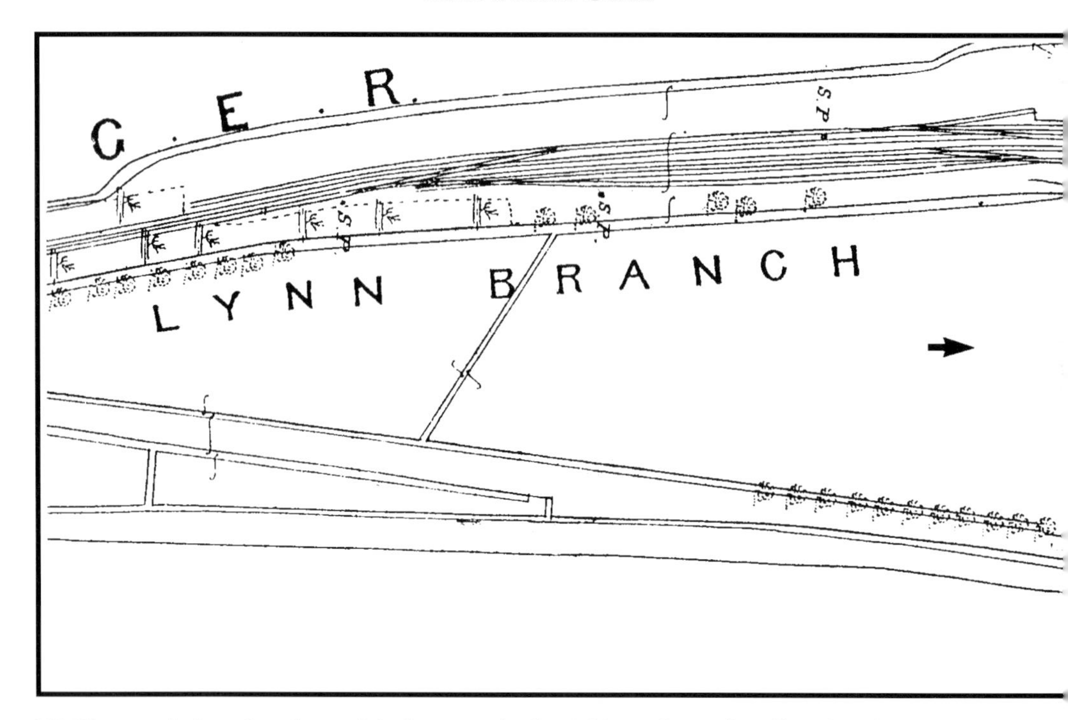

IV. The proximity of main road (subsequently the A10 trunk road), rail and major waterway are evident in this 1887 map. These facilities made Littleport a significant settlement in what was a sparsely populated area in the mid nineteenth century.

13. The main station building was an ornate structure, built mainly of flint although the platform elevation was faced with carstone, thus providing an unusual combination of local building materials from the areas east and north of the town. By contrast the waiting room on the easterly platform was a more modest wooden affair. Four railwaymen are trying to adopt natural poses for the cameramen in this picture, which dates from Great Eastern days. (Lens of Sutton)

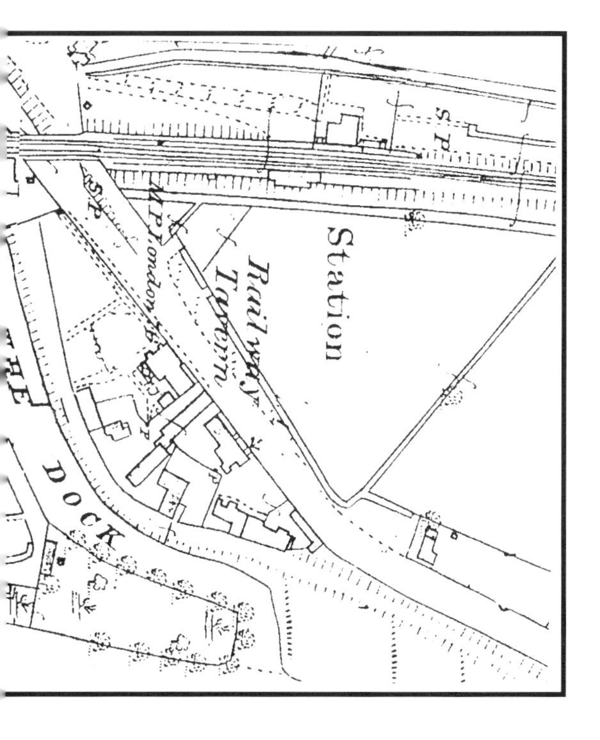

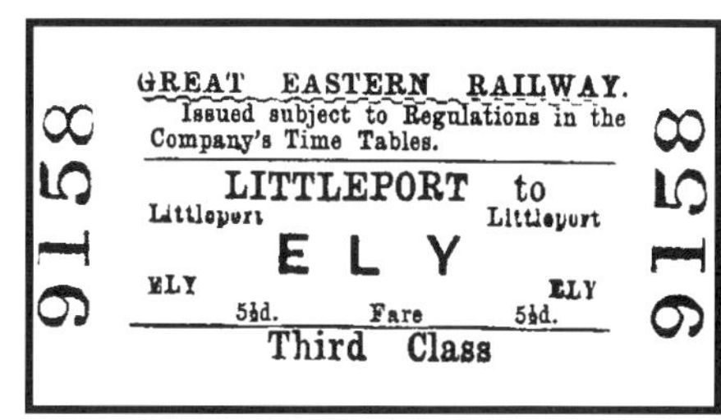

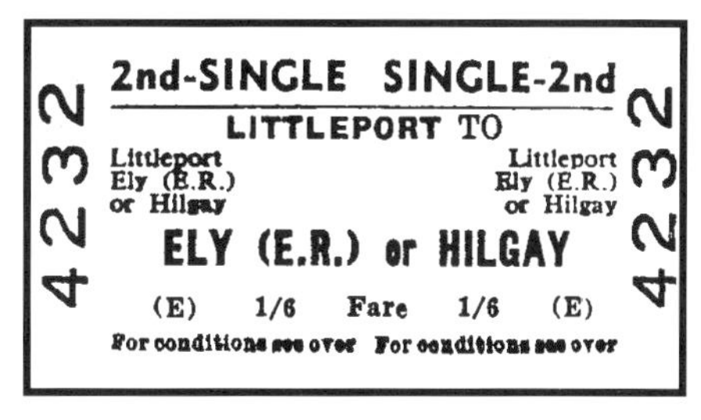

14. This view north-westwards from the signal box controlling access to the goods yard shows plenty of activity in the sidings, as sacks are loaded into the waiting wagons on an October day in 1911. The ground signals in front of the wagons are encased in iron frames to prevent them from being damaged by the shunting horses. As late as 1930 the LNER found it necessary to build two additional sidings on the west side of the yard to cope with the volume of traffic that was being handled. (HMRS, Hilton Collection)

15. An up train heads south, seemingly unaffected by the floods of January 1928, which have inundated the railway and surrounding countryside. The roof of the Yard signal box can be made out above the last coach. (Cambridgeshire Collection, Cambridge Central Library)

16. Pools of water lying between the tracks and a barrier of sandbags by the level crossing bear testimony to the disastrous floods of 1947 - a few days earlier, on 16th March, the floodwater had reached 14 inches above rail level at this point. The proximity of the Great Ouse made this section of the line particularly vulnerable to flooding. (Daily Herald)

17. The traditional signal box and more recent goods shed are reflected in the waters of the dock. This picture dates from 1957, by which time the siding to the dock had been lifted, but the loading gauge on the extreme left provides a clue as to where it once ran. (J.Watling collection)

18. At the south end of the station, impatient road users in vehicles less than 8'3" in height do not have to wait at the crossing gates when a train is due. This somewhat unusual duplication of level crossing and underbridge is also to be found at other locations in the region, such as Ely and Stonea. On a sunny March morning in 2000, a class 365 glides away from the station stop, passing the signal box, which has survived into the electrification era. (R.J.Adderson)

19. A handful of passengers gathers by the rudimentary shelter on the down platform as no.365533 arrives with a train from Kings Cross on the morning of 11th March 2000. The main station building has been demolished, and although the tall lamp standards and overhead wires are part of a modern railway, the shelter on the up platform provides a link with pre-grouping days. (R.J.Adderson)

NORTH OF LITTLEPORT

20. A class 47 approaches the station with the 07.42 from Kings Lynn to Liverpool Street on 24th June 1985. In the foreground, the bypass for the town is taking shape, making a scar across the countryside in much the same way as the infant railway had done 140 years earlier. Behind the bulldozer, the level crossing lights and barriers are already in operation, thus preventing any conflict between trains and contractors' vehicles. (D.C.Pearce)

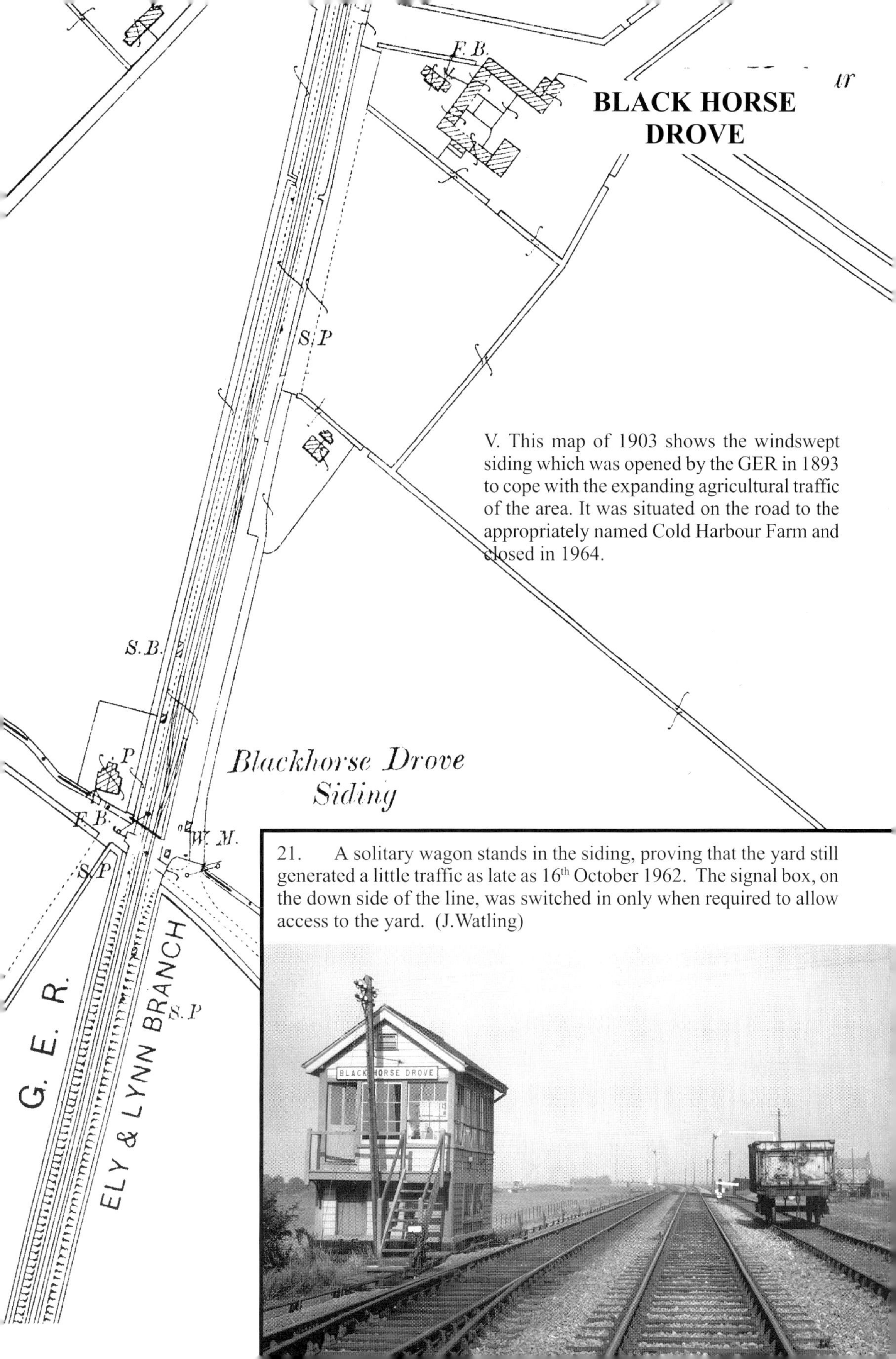

V. This map of 1903 shows the windswept siding which was opened by the GER in 1893 to cope with the expanding agricultural traffic of the area. It was situated on the road to the appropriately named Cold Harbour Farm and closed in 1964.

21. A solitary wagon stands in the siding, proving that the yard still generated a little traffic as late as 16th October 1962. The signal box, on the down side of the line, was switched in only when required to allow access to the yard. (J.Watling)

SOUTHERY

22. This siding, even more remote than that at Black Horse Drove, was opened in 1914 to serve extensive farmland owned by Sir Frederick Hiam: it survived until 1965. Initially, produce was brought in to the railhead by a horse-drawn narrow gauge tramway from the fens to the west. Looking north around 1960 we see the signal box on the east side of the line and the overgrown siding, with its concrete hard standing for road vehicles, on the west side. Gates at each end of the yard testify to its "private siding" status. (NRS Archive)

23. Here is the station looking northwards from the level crossing in 1927, showing the rather ill matched selection of buildings on the up side. There are one or two wagons in the siding behind the platform, but the wooden goods shed that used to stand here has already gone. (Stations UK)

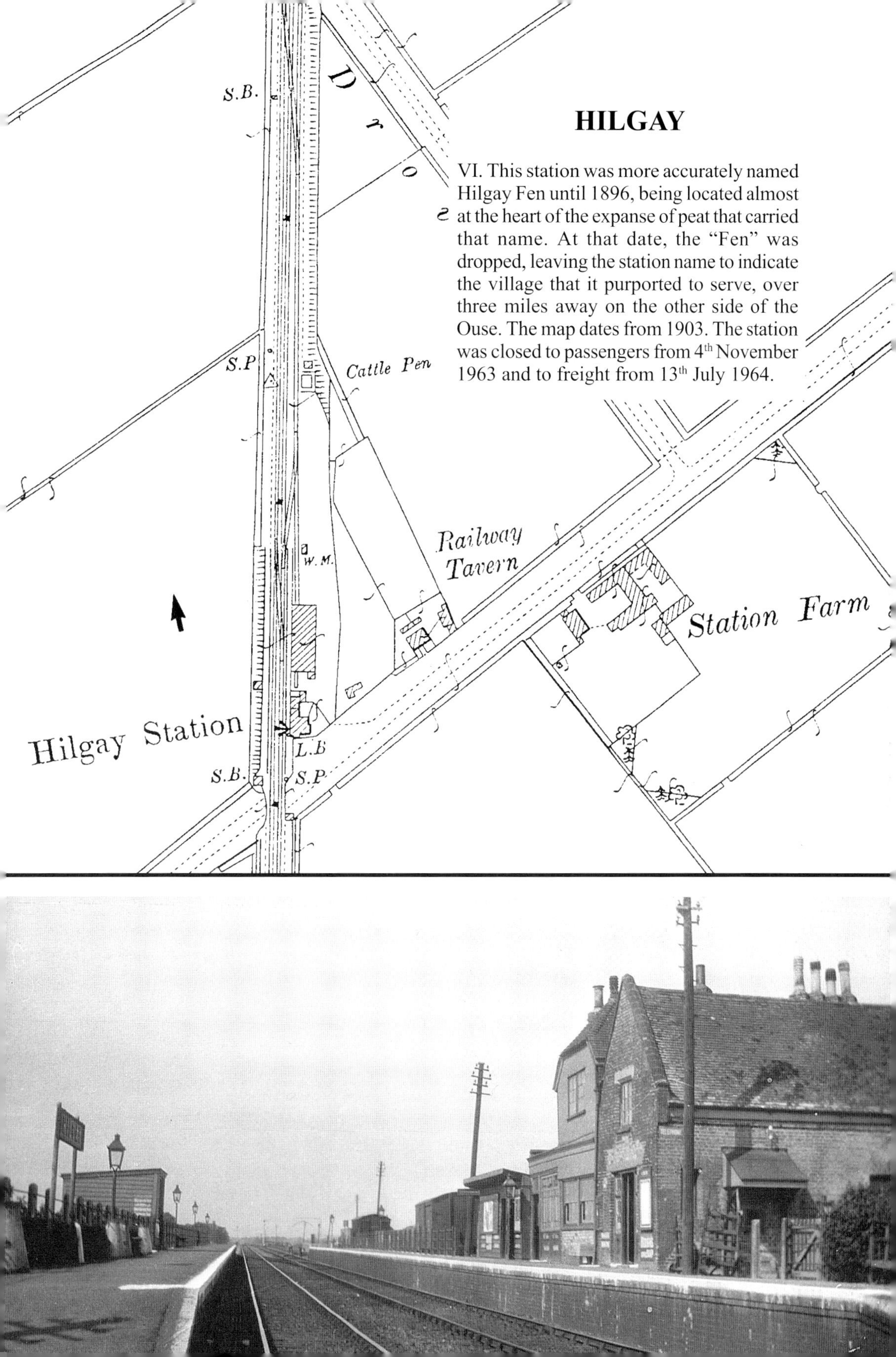

HILGAY

VI. This station was more accurately named Hilgay Fen until 1896, being located almost at the heart of the expanse of peat that carried that name. At that date, the "Fen" was dropped, leaving the station name to indicate the village that it purported to serve, over three miles away on the other side of the Ouse. The map dates from 1903. The station was closed to passengers from 4th November 1963 and to freight from 13th July 1964.

24. This remote spot hit the headlines in June 1939, when an up train collided with a lorry on Cross Drove occupation crossing, just north of the station. Before it could stop, the derailed train struck wagons in the adjacent goods siding, causing four fatalities and extensive damage. The incident was later attributed to gross carelessness on the part of the lorry driver, who had failed to see the approaching train despite clear visibility along the railway from the crossing. This was the scene of destruction just after the accident, showing the rear three coaches of the train. (Cambridge Daily News)

25. The locomotive involved was 4-4-0 no. 8783, one of two Kings Lynn based "Super Clauds" which were meticulously maintained in green livery for Royal train duties. It appears to have broken loose from the coaches before coming to rest at an angle of some 45 degrees just short of the platform. After being repaired the engine survived until the Summer of 1958, and we shall see it in happier circumstances in picture 103, bearing its later number of 2614. A remarkable feature of this picture is the number of people milling about on the tracks, many of whom appear by their clothing to be casual onlookers. (Cambridge Daily News)

26. Three railwaymen, probably the entire station staff, pose for a photograph by the nameboard in LNER days. Behind them the flat countryside stretches away to the distant horizon – apart from the odd farm, there is little habitation in this direction until one reaches March, some ten miles distant. (R.J.Adderson collection)

27. The neat topiary by the seat and the flowerbeds under the nameboard show how the railwaymen here filled some of the long hours between trains. Painted directions on the platform face provide an effective, if somewhat crude, guidance to would-be travellers. (R.J.Adderson collection)

28. Some flowers are still blooming on 16th October 1962, even though the railings could do with a bit of attention. The little waiting shed, projecting on stilts behind the down platform, looks somewhat insubstantial, but no doubt provided a welcome refuge for shoppers heading for Kings Lynn market on a wet and windy Tuesday morning. (J.Watling)

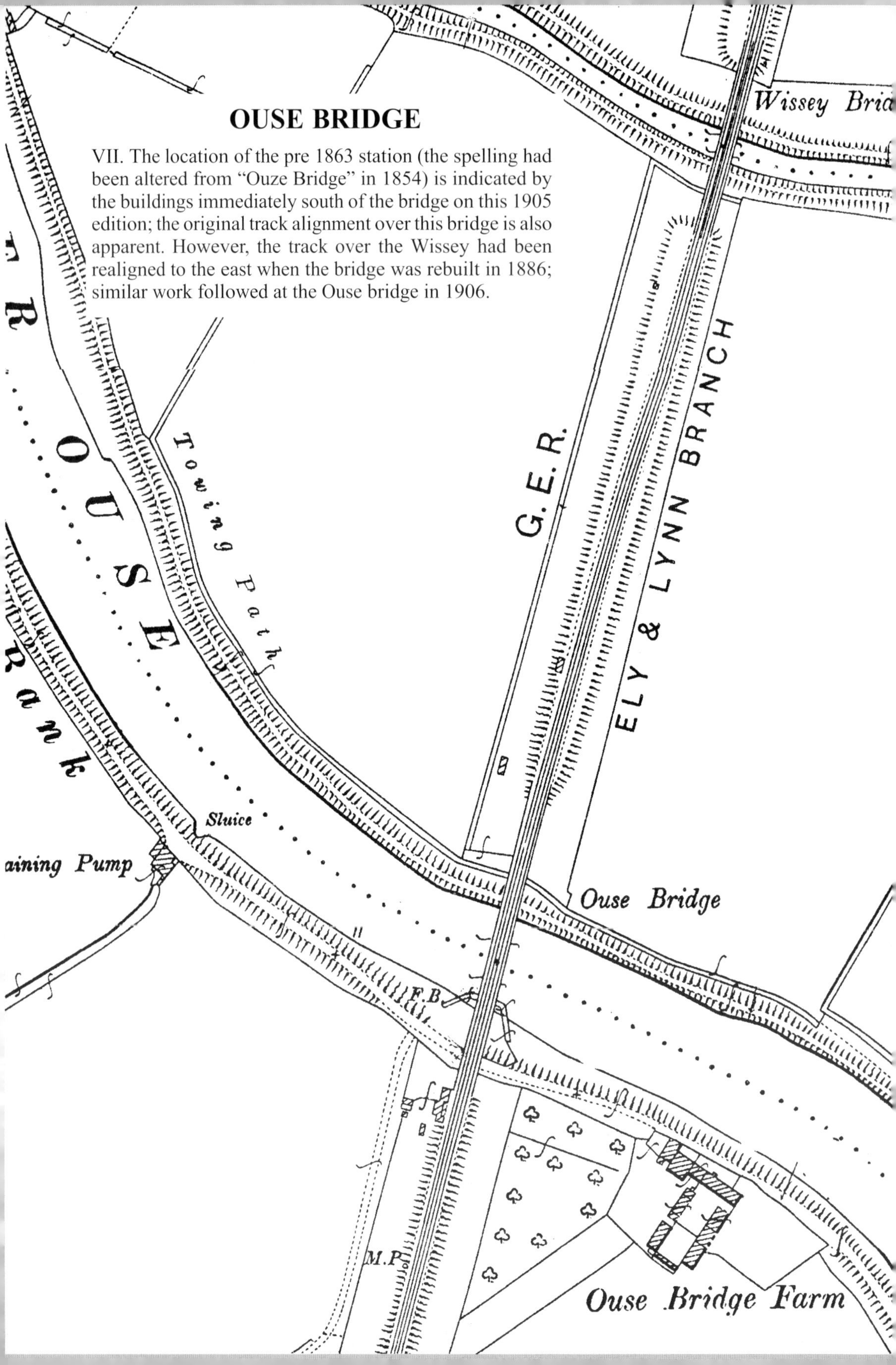

OUSE BRIDGE

VII. The location of the pre 1863 station (the spelling had been altered from "Ouze Bridge" in 1854) is indicated by the buildings immediately south of the bridge on this 1905 edition; the original track alignment over this bridge is also apparent. However, the track over the Wissey had been realigned to the east when the bridge was rebuilt in 1886; similar work followed at the Ouse bridge in 1906.

29. On the opening day, the first up train makes a special stop at the bridge, which was described by a contemporary commentator as "stupendous" and "an object of great curiosity to the passengers, who alighted from the train to examine its peculiar construction". Whilst the locomotives to the right are not greatly detailed, there is no reason to suppose that this is not an accurate representation of the bridge itself. (Illustrated London News)

30. Situated to the south of the road, the station at Ouse Bridge was closed as early as 1863. However some of the wooden buildings which we see here, raised on concrete pads owing to shrinkage of the surrounding fen, may date back to that time. A grimy D16/3 4-4-0 makes its way northwards with a passenger train, as army personnel assist with "mopping up" operations following the Winter flooding of 1947. (Cambridgeshire Collection, Cambridge Central Library)

31. As we look east along the river, no. 47579 *James Nightall G.C.* heads an up express over the "saddleback" steel girder bridge, which had replaced the original structure in 1906. All traces of the station had vanished by the time this picture was taken in April 1987. (R.J.Adderson)

32. In 1984 the line between Downham and Littleport had been reduced to single track, and this economy is apparent as a class 101 DMU crosses the bridge on an April day in 1990. Before long, the overhead wires would change the scene again. (J.Cordle)

33. A short distance north of the Ouse Bridge, a less than "stupendous" seven span bridge carries the railway across the River Wissey and the adjacent meadows. We are looking westwards along the bank of the river as a class 365 EMU speeds towards Downham on a fine Spring morning in March 2000. (R.J.Adderson)

CAMBRIDGE
L222

DENVER JUNCTION

VIII. This 1903 survey shows the original arrangement at the Junction when the branch was opened in 1882. We will return to the station after a trip down the branch to Stoke Ferry.

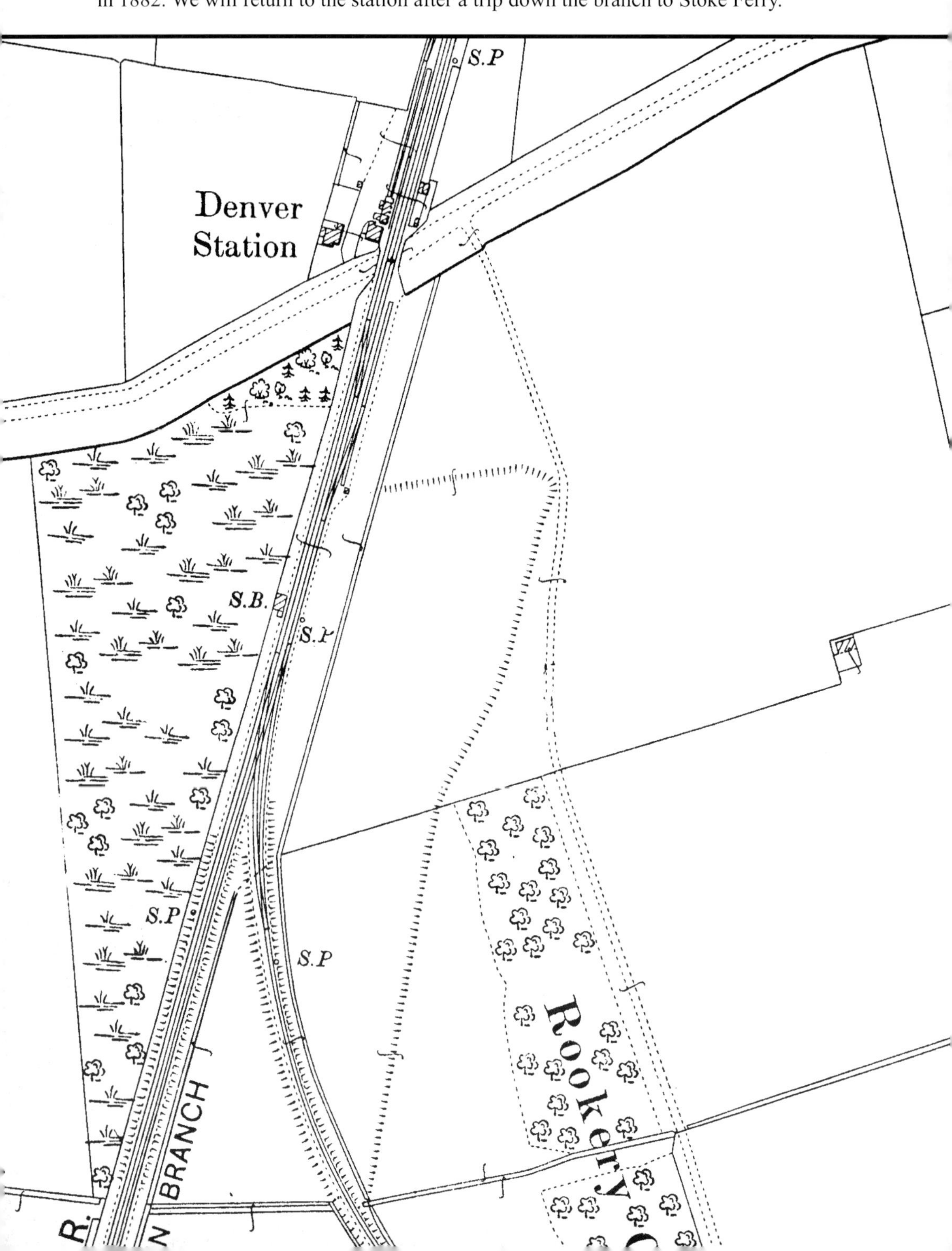

34. With the Stoke Ferry branch line diverging to the right, no. 37041 heads south past the junction with a sand train from Middleton Towers on 29th March 1980. Since 1932 the little signal box had been used only when there was traffic on the branch or the station sidings, and the track layout which it controlled had been simplified with the removal of the double junction to the branch (as shown on the map) in 1951. (D.C.Pearce)

35. The shiny rails show that all trains used the old up line south of Denver and the former down line to the north after single line working was introduced between Littleport and Downham. A wagon load of track panels beyond the signal post testifies to track lifting operations further north, and the rusting branch and down main tracks will soon be removed, as will the signal box, which no longer serves any useful purpose. This poignant summary of the decline of the traditional railway was recorded from the cab of a down express in late July 1985. (D.C.Pearce)

2. Stoke Ferry Branch

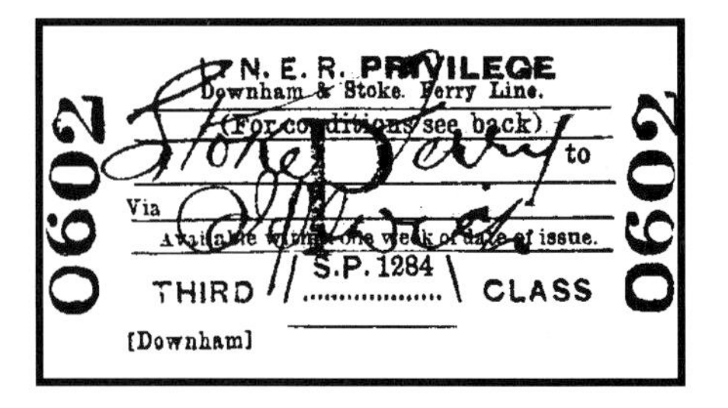

An unusual "blank" ticket printed specifically for use on the branch. This one was used on the penultimate up working on the last day of passenger services in September 1930. (G.Croughton)

RYSTON

IX. This station, which served a combined 1881 population of 238 in the parishes of Fordham, Ryston and Roxham, undoubtedly owed its existence to the proximity of Ryston Hall, the seat of the Pratt family whose head was Lord of the Manor. The presence, on this 1905 map of a siding designated "Squires Siding", which on another edition was shown as "Pratt's Siding" testifies to their influence. It was originally intended to use the name of the largest parish, Fordham, but this was probably changed to avoid confusion with a station of the same name in Cambridgeshire. The simple layout provided was adequate for dealing with any eventuality for the whole of the station's life. After implementation of "Light Railway" status following withdrawal of the passenger service, the level crossing was the only one to retain gates. Freight traffic continued officially until 28th December 1964.

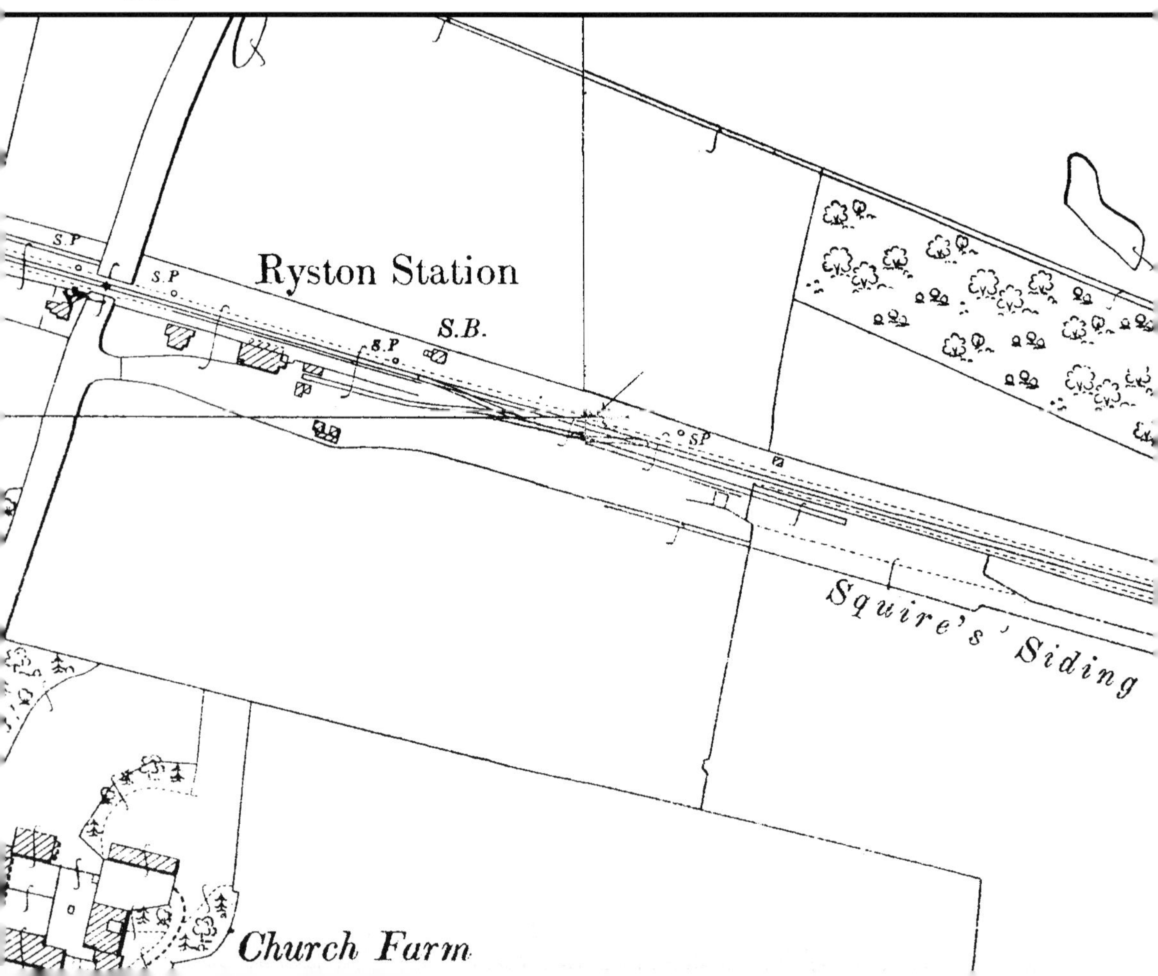

36. The station was fully signalled and the branch still had a passenger service when this picture was taken around 1925, looking along the line towards Stoke Ferry. On the right is the station house, but the station building on the platform is partially obscured by foliage. (Stations UK)

37. Some thirty-five years later, the Summer leaves have given way to the bare boughs of winter, allowing us a full view of the station building. The signalling has gone, of course, but little else has changed: the hedge is cut to exactly the same contours and the upstairs window is open to exactly the same extent! (Stations UK)

38. Having visited Mildenhall and its old M&GN haunts at East Rudham earlier in the day, Ivatt class 4 2-6-0 no. 43149 stands at the east end of the station with an enthusiast's special on 26th May 1962. This was one of several such railtours to travel over the branch after the passenger closure, and the last to be steam-hauled. (R.J.Adderson)

ABBEY & WEST DEREHAM

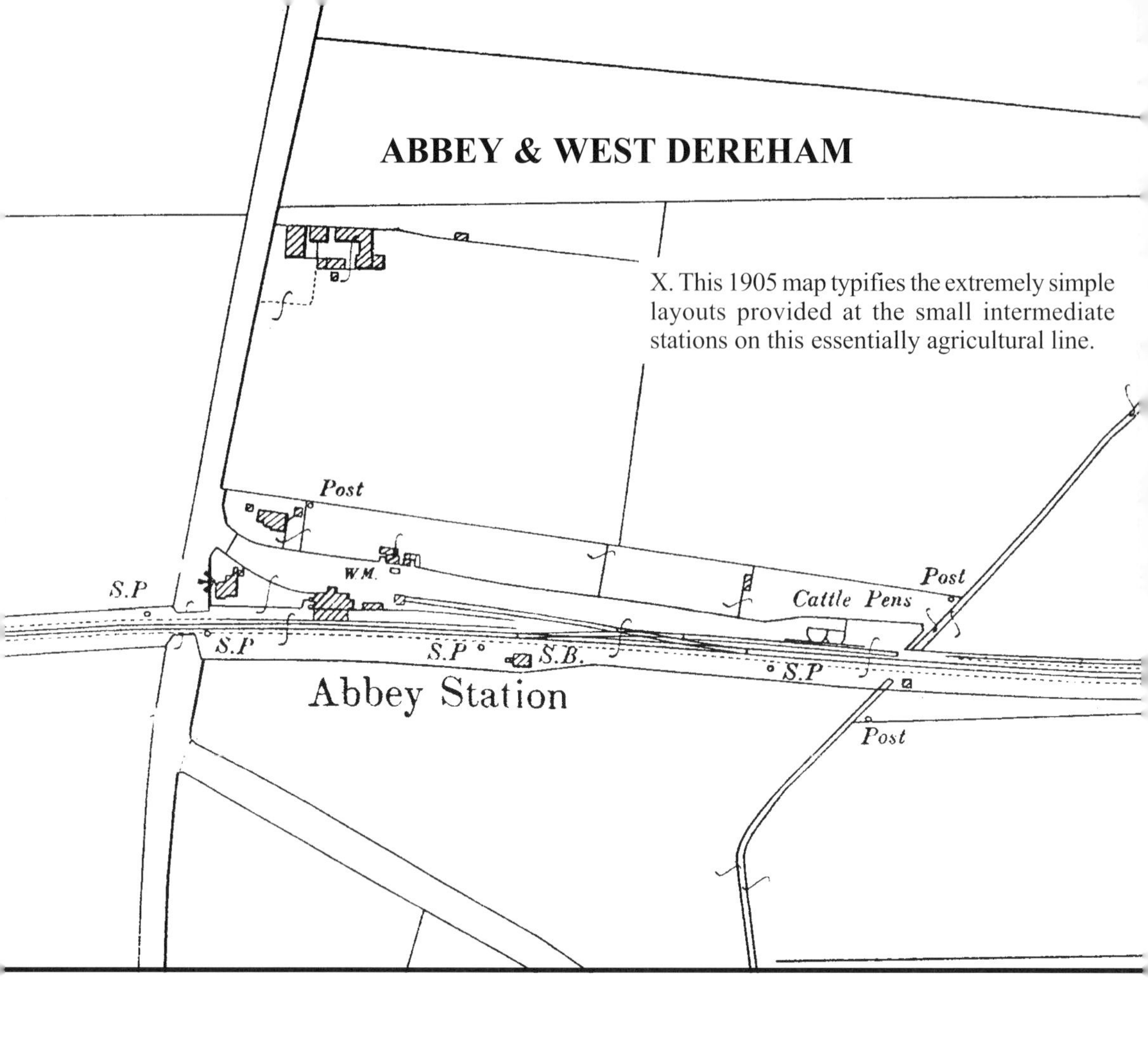

X. This 1905 map typifies the extremely simple layouts provided at the small intermediate stations on this essentially agricultural line.

39. Unusually, the station was originally named after a nearby farm, and it had been open for some years before the name of the nearby village of West Dereham was added to the title. The girl's clothing suggests that this picture dates from the late Victorian era. Although the station building is fairly basic, substantial two-storey houses were provided here for both the stationmaster and crossing keeper. (Lens of Sutton)

40. Looking towards the station from the east in 1911, we have a glimpse of the short-lived signal box on the left, together with some of the signals that it controlled. In the siding, sacks are being transferred between a horse-drawn cart and an open railway wagon. The stationmaster's house can be seen above the cart. (HMRS, Hilton Collection)

41. The canopy was removed after the passenger service was withdrawn, and the building was looking quite bare when this photograph was taken from the level crossing on 15th April 1965. However, there are a few wagons in the siding, and the branch goods train is pottering around on the running line. The vicious looking cattle grid provides a challenge to would-be modellers. (G.R.Croughton)

42. No. D5655 stands at the platform on Thursday, 15th April 1965, having detached two empty wagons bound for Wissington beet factory. The engine and brake van will now form the last ever train over the next three miles to Stoke Ferry. Although there are no wagons to set down or pick up at the terminus, the train still has to perform the important task of delivering the final wages packets to the staff there. (G.R.Croughton)

KEEBLE'S SIDING

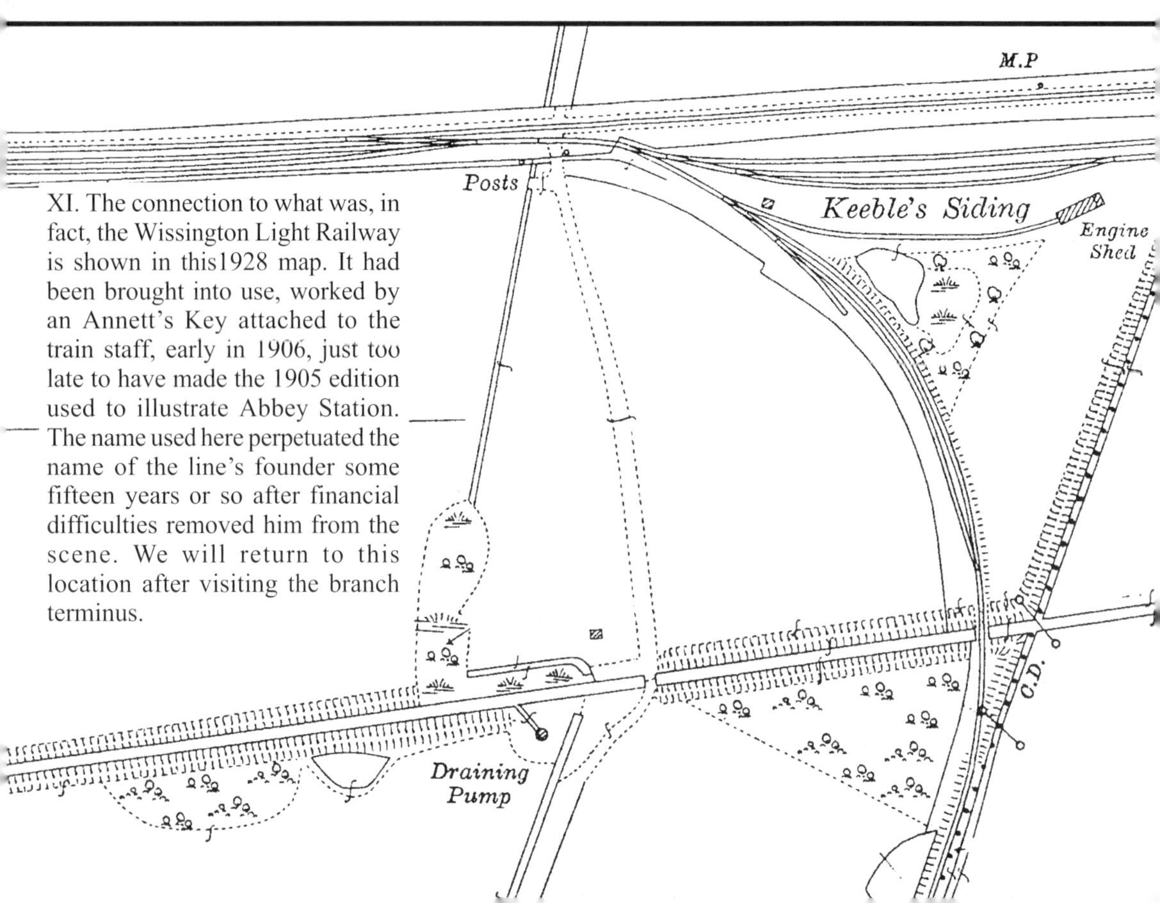

XI. The connection to what was, in fact, the Wissington Light Railway is shown in this1928 map. It had been brought into use, worked by an Annett's Key attached to the train staff, early in 1906, just too late to have made the 1905 edition used to illustrate Abbey Station. The name used here perpetuated the name of the line's founder some fifteen years or so after financial difficulties removed him from the scene. We will return to this location after visiting the branch terminus.

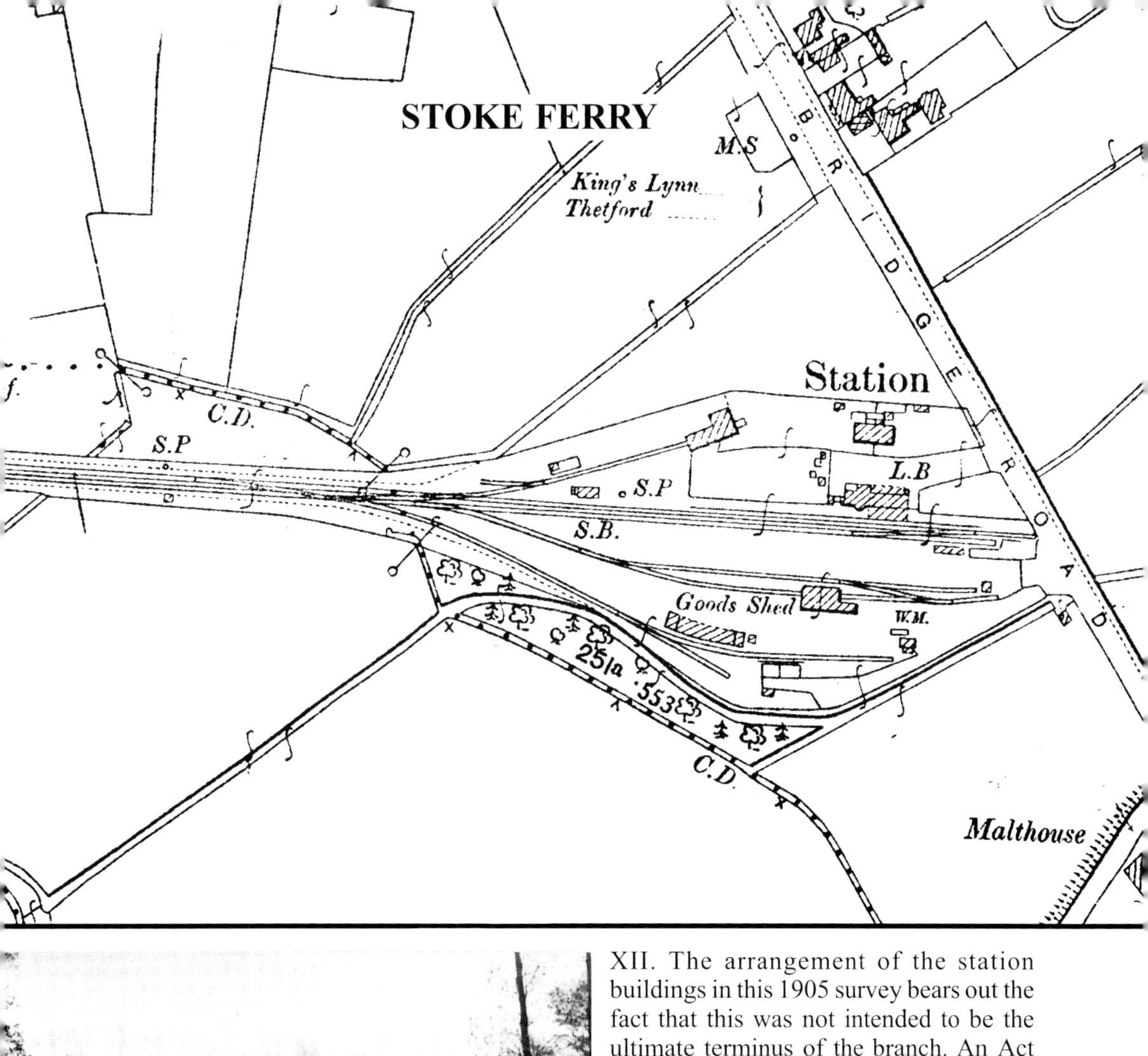

XII. The arrangement of the station buildings in this 1905 survey bears out the fact that this was not intended to be the ultimate terminus of the branch. An Act was passed in 1883 for an extension to Gooderstone but plans were formally abandoned by another Act of 1887 after disappointing receipts on the initial line.

43. The down home signal provides an excellent vantage point for the photographer as he looks eastwards along the lines into the station on 10th November 1911. (HMRS, Hilton Collection)

44. The importance of the railway to the local economy in the years before World War 1 is emphasised by the activity in the goods yard on the same day. Behind the railwayman is the somewhat rickety coal shed, whilst general freight traffic would be handled in the substantial brick goods shed at the far end of the yard. (HMRS, Hilton Collection)

45. Now the photographer has moved a few yards backwards and to his left to record, from left to right, the water tower, loco shed, station houses, signal box and passenger platform. It would seem that the shed line is being used as an overflow from the goods yard. The apparently top-heavy sheeted wagon on the right is loaded with hay – a similar load appears in picture 40. (HMRS, Hilton Collection)

46. Although the goods traffic was enough to keep the terminus open into the 1960s, the passenger trains never thrived. This portrait of the deserted station in the last years of the passenger service sums it all up – the only sign of life is a horse waiting patiently for something to happen. The platform canopy has been removed since the 1911 picture. (J.Watling collection)

47. By contrast, the same viewpoint shows the platform and yard swarming with humanity on 12th July 1959, as class J69 0-6-0T no. 68566 runs round the LCGB "Eastern Counties Limited" railtour. Removal of the point rodding has revealed the brick arches on which the platform was built owing to the unstable nature of the land here. (A.E.Bennett)

WISSINGTON LIGHT RAILWAY

XIII. This simplified map illustrates the extensive nature of the railway as it sought to serve all corners of this fertile fenland area. (R.Darsley/Industrial Railway Society)

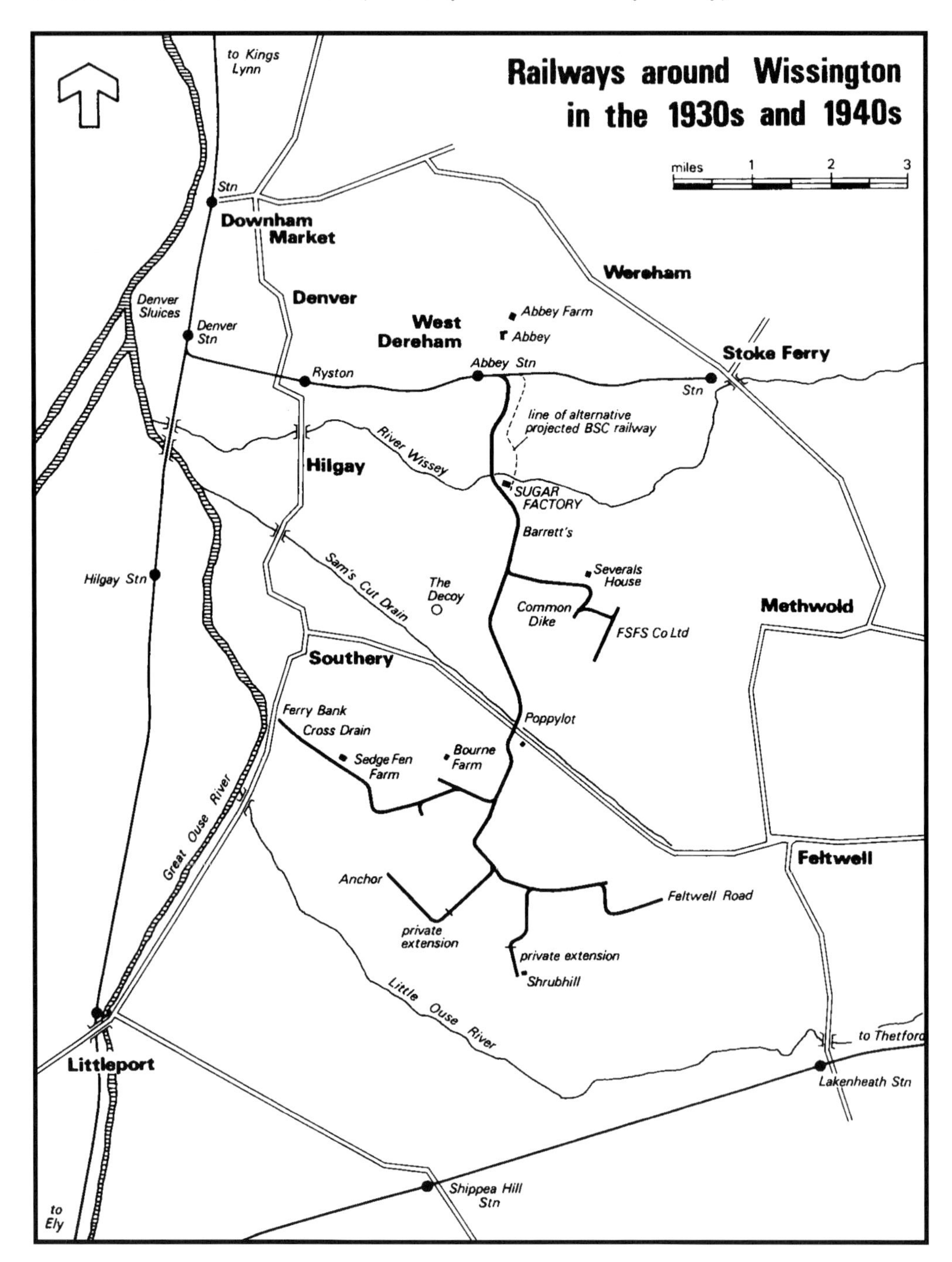

48. We now return to Abbey for a trip down the Wissington Light Railway. Here is the junction between the Stoke Ferry branch and what was then referred to as Keeble's siding on a Winter day in 1911. Abbey station is beyond the ground frame hut by the buffer stops. (HMRS, Hilton Collection)

49. Manning Wardle 0-6-0ST *Newcastle* approaches the junction with the Stoke Ferry line on 22nd November 1964. To the right, the line to the beet factory curves sharply away southwards, whilst the points lead to the exchange sidings. The prohibition notice refers to main line engines; Wissington Railway locos regularly worked on BR metals in this area. (R.C.Riley)

50. Some six weeks earlier *Wissington* had ventured into the neglected exchange sidings with a lengthy train. This locomotive, a Hudswell Clark 0-6-0ST, had been delivered new to the factory in 1938, and was moved to the North Norfolk Railway in 1978 after withdrawal. In 1999 it made a nostalgic return to the factory, albeit on the back of a lorry, on its way to a complete overhaul. (Ivo Peters)

51. By the following autumn, the exchange sidings had virtually disappeared in the long grass. On this occasion, it is *Newcastle* that has braved the undergrowth during a Norfolk Railway Society visit on 24th October 1965, and the Society's President, Norwich shedmaster Bill Harvey, is leaning from the cab. It is a far cry from his normal day-to-day railway activities! (R.J.Adderson)

52. *Wissington* crosses the modern concrete bridge spanning the Cut-off Channel with empty wagons bound for Abbey on 6th October 1964. Although inward beet traffic ceased by the mid 1960s, the railway continued to handle oil, coke and limestone for the factory. The Channel, an entirely new waterway over 25 miles in length, had been cut a few years earlier to improve the drainage of the area. (Ivo Peters)

53. With the beet factory in the background, *Wissington* heads a train of empties over the elevated section of track leading to the bridge over the River Wissey on 8th May 1964. (R.C.Riley)

54. The photographer captures a tranquil moment with three locomotives resting in the factory sidings on 6th October 1964. *Wissington* stands in front of *Newcastle*, whilst the trio is completed by another Manning Wardle 0-6-0ST, No 2006,which dates back to 1921. (Ivo Peters)

55. Steam from both the factory and the loco is whipped away by the bitter wind, as *Mac*, a work-stained Hudswell Clark 0-4-0ST, busies itself in the factory complex in the early 1950s. Built in 1899, *Mac* was sold to British Sugar Manufacturing Limited after being used by the contractors building the factory, and survived until 1957. This industrial atmosphere contrasts vividly with the deserted countryside we have experienced on our journey from Ely. (Eastern Counties Newspapers)

56. Steam traction monopolised the railway until 1965, when a brand new John Fowler 0-4-0 diesel hydraulic arrived. The newcomer stands on the line leading to its shed on 24th October 1965. (R.J.Adderson)

←

57. The factory expanded greatly over the years, and by the end of the twentieth century it had become the largest sugar beet factory in Europe. A new silo was under construction in the Summer of 1969, dwarfing one of the little saddle tanks. By way of contrast, the ancient flat-bottomed track in the foreground almost certainly dates back to the early days of the railway. To the right of the brick hut, the track is interlaced over the weighbridge, allowing easier movement for vehicles not requiring to be weighed. (R.F.Bonny)

58. Here we have a scene of great activity on one of the lines that wandered off across the featureless fenland south of the factory. The men fork the crop into the waiting wagons, as the ladies take a rest from the back-breaking chore of topping the beet. Meanwhile, one of the saddle tanks blows off impatiently, ready to take another load to the factory for processing on a fine winters day in the 1950s. (Eastern Counties Newspapers)

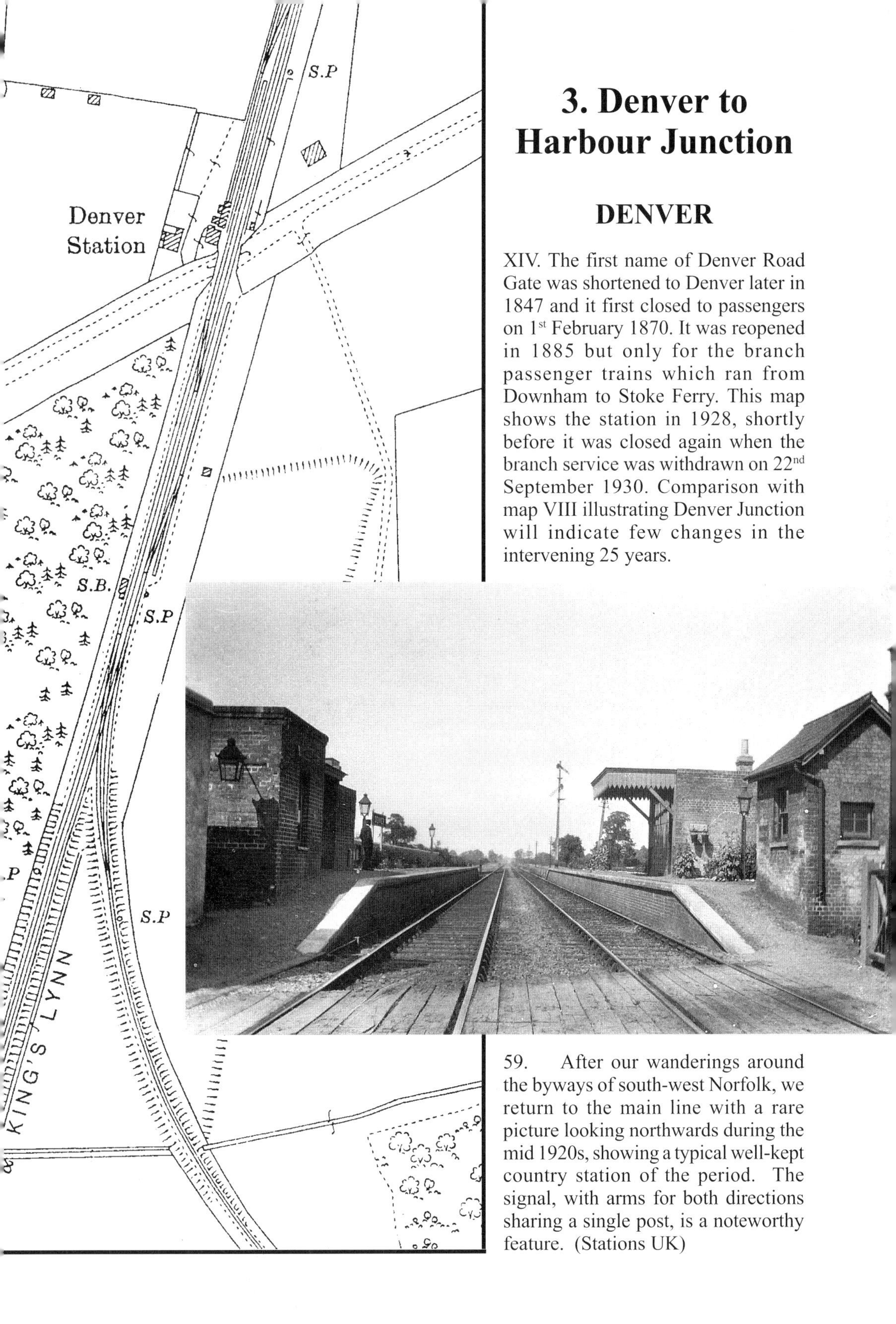

3. Denver to Harbour Junction

DENVER

XIV. The first name of Denver Road Gate was shortened to Denver later in 1847 and it first closed to passengers on 1st February 1870. It was reopened in 1885 but only for the branch passenger trains which ran from Downham to Stoke Ferry. This map shows the station in 1928, shortly before it was closed again when the branch service was withdrawn on 22nd September 1930. Comparison with map VIII illustrating Denver Junction will indicate few changes in the intervening 25 years.

59. After our wanderings around the byways of south-west Norfolk, we return to the main line with a rare picture looking northwards during the mid 1920s, showing a typical well-kept country station of the period. The signal, with arms for both directions sharing a single post, is a noteworthy feature. (Stations UK)

60. Thirty years later, the up platform has lost its fire buckets, lamp and waiting room awning, but the structure has changed little as Class D16/3 4-4-0 no. 62530 heads an up stopping train through the closed station. The exposed ground frame in the foreground suggests that the crossing keeper's job could be an unenviable one on a cold Winter night! (Stations UK)

61. At much the same time, another D16/3 heads a down train over the level crossing past the station house which is built of the distinctive local carstone. Apart from the motive power, this scene would remain virtually unchanged until the 1980s, when the line was singled and the crossing automated. (Stations UK)

62. Another ten years have rolled by, as we share the guard's view southwards through the platforms from the brake van of a goods train on April 15th 1965. The goods siding can be seen beyond the level crossing, with the branch striking off to the left by the junction signal. (G.R.Croughton)

63. A trainload of imported Polish coal, running from Kings Lynn docks to Foxton, takes the one remaining track through the overgrown platforms in November 1992. This twice-weekly train was a favourite with local enthusiasts because of the variety of locomotive power used, and on this occasion they would have been delighted to see no. 31165 *Stratford Major Depot*, which had been repainted in its original green livery. (J.Cordle)

Station
BENNETT STREET
Mills
Timber Yard
Saw Pit
Kilns
Brick Wo
Station
Eagle Mills
(Flour)
Goods Shed
Malthouse
P.H.
P.O.
BENNETT STREET
VICTORIA

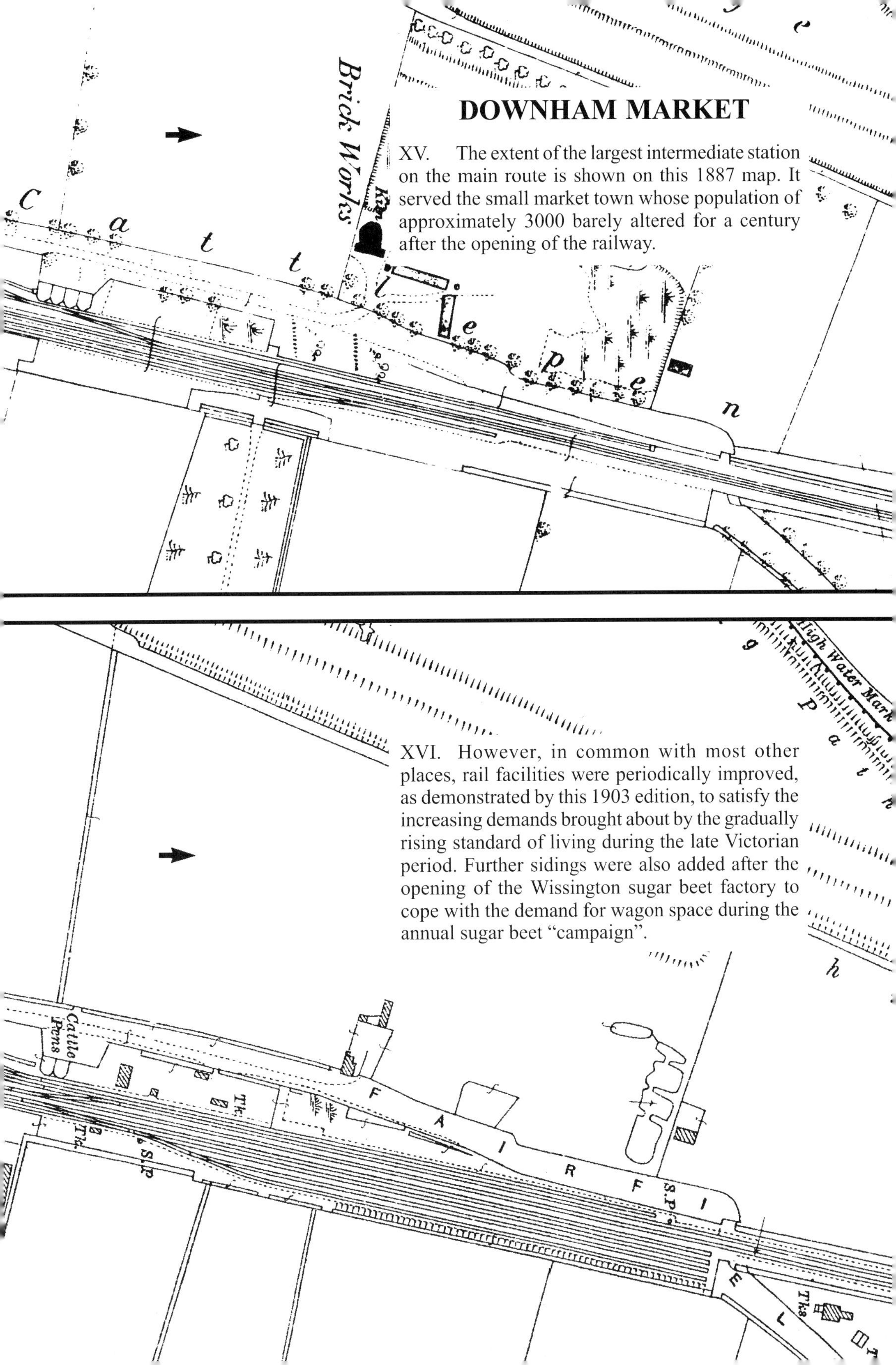

DOWNHAM MARKET

XV. The extent of the largest intermediate station on the main route is shown on this 1887 map. It served the small market town whose population of approximately 3000 barely altered for a century after the opening of the railway.

XVI. However, in common with most other places, rail facilities were periodically improved, as demonstrated by this 1903 edition, to satisfy the increasing demands brought about by the gradually rising standard of living during the late Victorian period. Further sidings were also added after the opening of the Wissington sugar beet factory to cope with the demand for wagon space during the annual sugar beet “campaign”.

64. During the GER era, we see passengers awaiting the arrival of an up train, which can just be made out at the far end of the platform. The water tank continued to dominate the south end of the platform until the early 1960s; the signal box survived all the changes to remain in use in 2000. (G.L.Kenworthy collection)

65. Looking north from the up starter signal, the photographer has captured a busy moment on 10th November 1911. The activity on the short up platform suggests that a train is due, and men are busy in the goods yard, unloading railway wagons into horse-drawn carts. An unattended horse box stands at the down platform, whilst a plume of steam in the distant up sidings probably indicates the presence of the Stoke Ferry train, tucked out of the way until its next jaunt along the branch. Earlier in the year, the down platform had been extended northwards, and the freshly painted fencing at the far end clearly marks the new construction. (HMRS, Hilton Collection)

66. There were sidings on each side of the running lines at both ends of the station. We are looking through the goods shed at the south end towards the station and level crossing on 2nd February 1966. (J.Watling)

67. As we see from the map, a wagon turntable in the north-east yard gave access to a siding running at right angles to the main line to serve an adjacent mill. Here is this little-photographed feature of the railway scene, again on 2nd February 1966, with the main line connection coming in from the left and the mill line heading off to the right. Perhaps unnecessarily, a notice prohibited engines from running on to this contraption. (J.Watling)

68. Smoke drifts lazily from the signal box chimney, as we look southwards from the up platform on the same February day. Since the installation of wheel-operated level crossing gates in 1937, there had been no need for the signalman to leave the warmth of his box to swing the gates by hand. The bulk of Eagle Mill, with a wagon in the siding, dominates the background, whilst the distant gasworks, dating back to 1875, also had its private siding. A comparison with the next picture will emphasise how the little the infrastructure changed until the track rationalisation of the mid-1980s. (J.Watling)

69. From much the same viewpoint we see no. 47016 as it slows for the station stop with the 08.36 train from Liverpool Street on 1st May 1982. There are only detail changes from the previous picture - lifting barriers had replaced the traditional level crossing gates in 1975, the up sidings beyond the crossing have been removed, and, away from the railway, the Mill windows have been double glazed. The signal box nameboard reflects the official change of the station name to Downham **Market**, a renaming which appeared in the timetables from 1st June 1981 following a request from the local council. (D.C.Pearce)

70. Although freight traffic over the route declined gradually from the 1960s onwards, the daily sand trains from Middleton Towers have run consistently over the years. Nos 37354 and 37218 stand at the platform with the loaded train on 10th April 1990, waiting for a path over the single track southwards to Littleport. The main station buildings, again built largely of the local carstone, are still well maintained. (R.J.Adderson)

71. In his report on the opening of the line, a local newspaper reporter described the station building as a "chaste erection". Over 150 years later, he would have had little problem in recognising the structure, although he would probably have chosen different words to describe it! On a March morning in 2000 the absence of parked cars on the approach road enables us to appreciate the thorough and sympathetic refurbishment which had taken place a decade or so earlier. (R.J.Adderson)

STOW BARDOLPH

XVII. Road bridges across the Ouse between Ely and Kings Lynn were few; that provided here at Stow Bridge connected two portions of a geographically large parish, divided by the Ouse, and provided an obvious location for a station. "Bardolph" was added to the station name following the Grouping of 1923 to distinguish it from Stow on the former North British Railway, south of Edinburgh; the suffix was retained until closure, on the same day as Hilgay in 1963. The map dates from 1903.

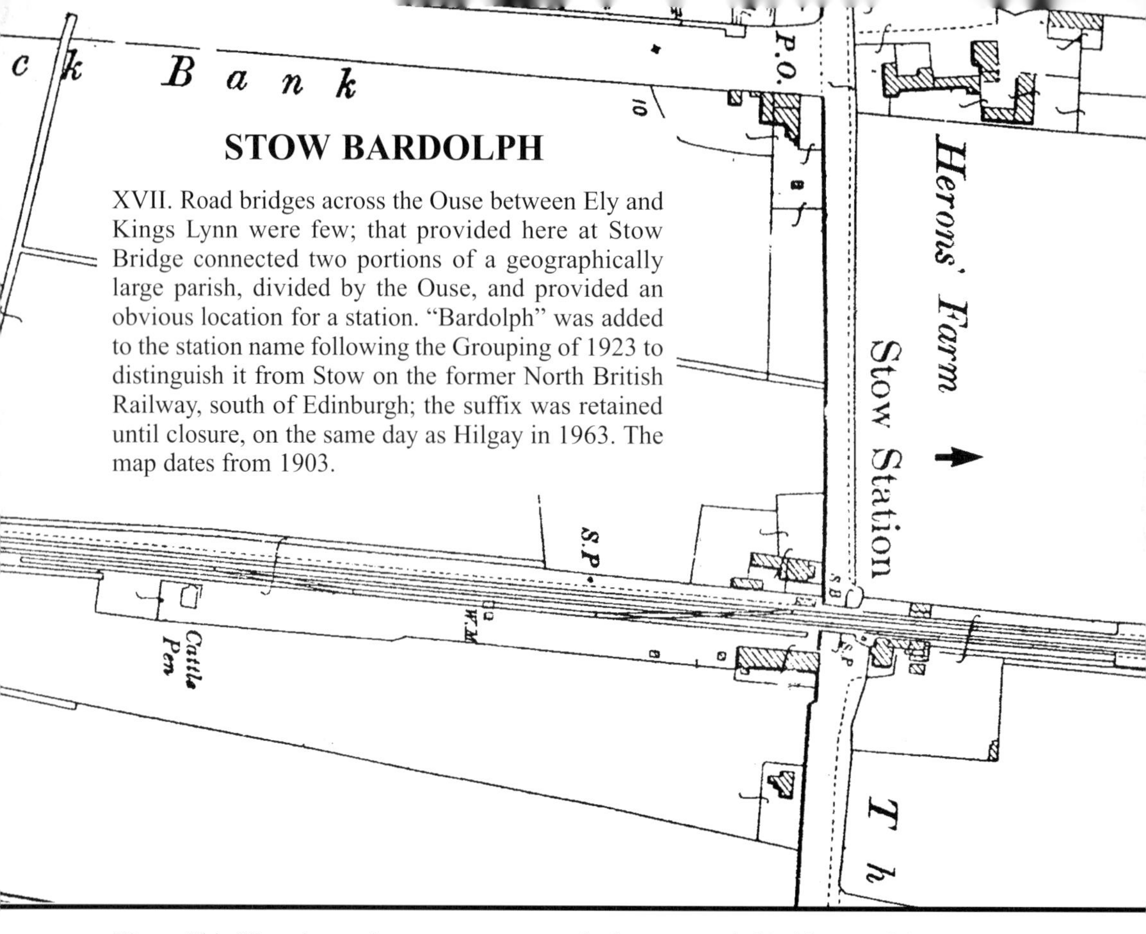

72. This Victorian outing was a rare event in the unremarkable history of the station. It seems to have been as much a social occasion as a technical one when the tiny *Gazelle* called in the course of a trial trip from Kings Lynn to Downham and back on 5th February 1893. The engine had been built by Dodman's at Kings Lynn for the private use of William Burkitt, a one-time mayor of the town and director of the Docks and Railway Company. Much rebuilt over the years, it survived a spell on the Shropshire and Montgomeryshire Railway before being preserved on the Longmoor Military Railway. After some years at Beverley, it was moved to Tenterden in the late 1990s. (Dr T.F.Budden, Jack Braithwaite Collection, courtesy M&GN Circle)

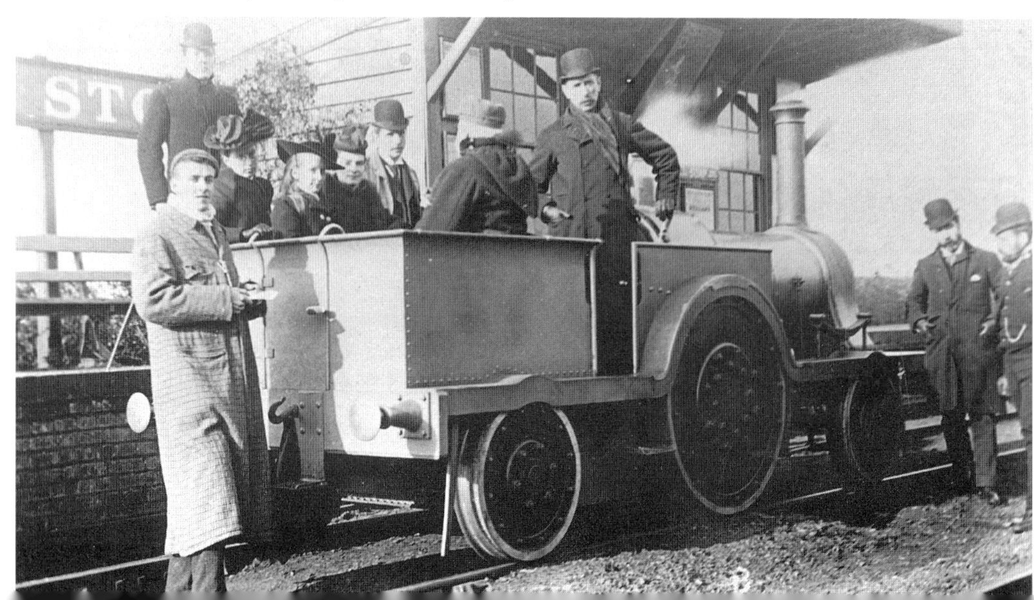

73. The signalman's outlook northwards along the platforms in the late 1930s shows that here, too the main station building was built from carstone. Next to it is the shelter and waiting room which were provided as the result of local pressure in 1875 – the engineer was authorised to spend £25 to provide these facilities. In the previous year the gross receipts here totalled £1609.8.11d, so no doubt the expenditure could be justified. However, as at Denver, we can see that the Great Eastern Railway had been economical in their use of signal posts! (Stations UK)

74. Preserved class A3 4-6-2 no. 4472 *"Flying Scotsman"* worked a number of trains over the line as part of the "Fenline Steam Weekend" of 19th-20th October 1991. With the former station building on the right, the distinguished visitor heads south under the electrification wires. (D.C.Pearce)

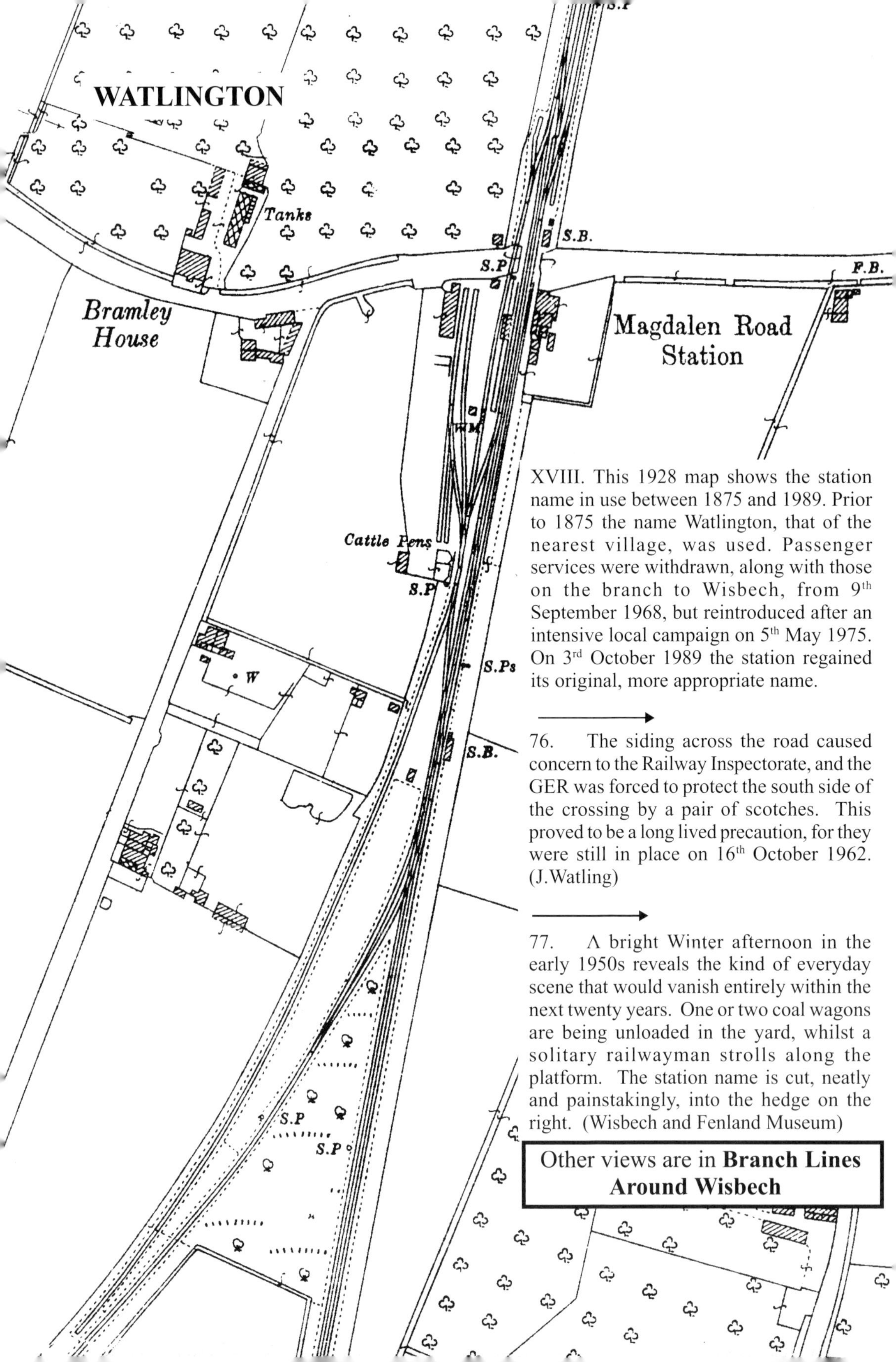

XVIII. This 1928 map shows the station name in use between 1875 and 1989. Prior to 1875 the name Watlington, that of the nearest village, was used. Passenger services were withdrawn, along with those on the branch to Wisbech, from 9th September 1968, but reintroduced after an intensive local campaign on 5th May 1975. On 3rd October 1989 the station regained its original, more appropriate name.

76. The siding across the road caused concern to the Railway Inspectorate, and the GER was forced to protect the south side of the crossing by a pair of scotches. This proved to be a long lived precaution, for they were still in place on 16th October 1962. (J.Watling)

77. A bright Winter afternoon in the early 1950s reveals the kind of everyday scene that would vanish entirely within the next twenty years. One or two coal wagons are being unloaded in the yard, whilst a solitary railwayman strolls along the platform. The station name is cut, neatly and painstakingly, into the hedge on the right. (Wisbech and Fenland Museum)

Other views are in **Branch Lines Around Wisbech**

75. The extent, if not the detail, of the station is well shown in this view southwards from a signal post in November 1911. On the right is the goods yard, whilst a set of inward-opening gates is provided at the point where the down siding crosses the road. In 1928 a new signal box, with wheel operated gates, was built on the east side of the line just north of the level crossing. (HMRS, Hilton Collection)

78. Looking south from the end of the up platform in late 1959, we see the line from March and Wisbech curving in from the right. Class J19 0-6-0 no.64665 is shunting in the yard, and presumably no northbound trains are due for some time, as it has left part of its train on the down main line. (NRS Archive)

79. No. 47576 *Kings Lynn* slows for the station stop with an up train on 28th April 1990. Although by this time the station had been renamed "Watlington", the signal box nameboard still read "Magdalen Road" – an apparent inconsistency that would continue into the 21st century. (R.J.Adderson)

80. Here is the signalman's view of the replacement up platform, which was built north of the level crossing during the early 1990s. In April 1992 it appears to be structurally complete, although the lighting has yet to be installed. No 47377 has just left the single track section with a block train of grain bound for Burghead in Morayshire – a traffic flow which was subsequently lost to coastal shipping. (J.Cordle)

81. We turn to look southwards from the signal box on the same day, and see a single passenger alighting from the 3-car diesel unit, which will soon be replaced by electric trains. Although it has lost its canopy, the narrow waiting room on the down platform continues to provide inspiration to space-starved railway modellers. Sadly, it was to be replaced by a modern glass structure a few years later. (J.Cordle)

ST.GERMANS

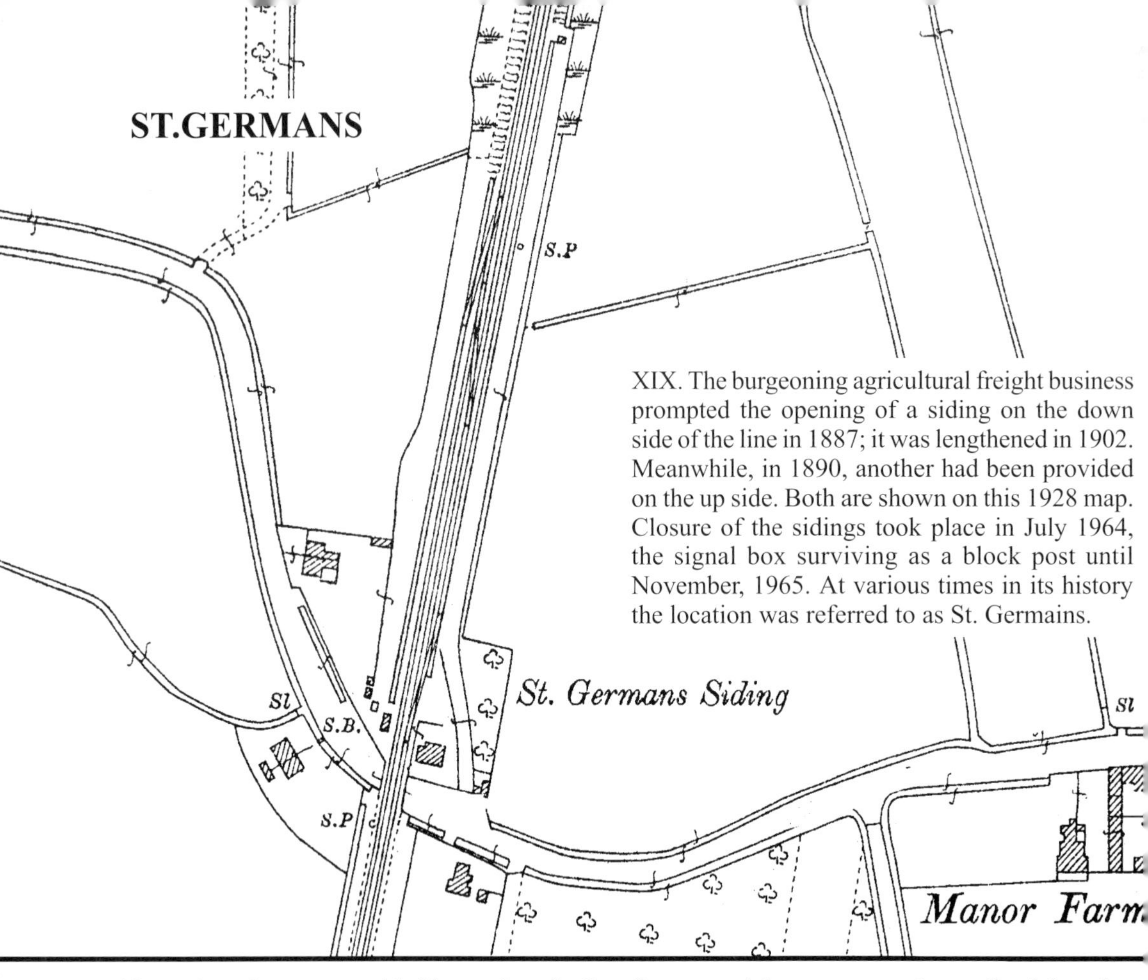

XIX. The burgeoning agricultural freight business prompted the opening of a siding on the down side of the line in 1887; it was lengthened in 1902. Meanwhile, in 1890, another had been provided on the up side. Both are shown on this 1928 map. Closure of the sidings took place in July 1964, the signal box surviving as a block post until November, 1965. At various times in its history the location was referred to as St. Germains.

82. A station was provided here when the line first opened, but was even shorter lived than that at Ouse Bridge, as it disappeared from the timetables in 1850. Its closure almost certainly resulted from the involvement of the Official Receiver at that time. Looking south on 22nd April 1967, we see that the original station building, which bears a marked similarity to that at Stow, is still standing, whilst the signal box remains to control the crossing gates. (J.Watling)

CLARKE'S DROVE

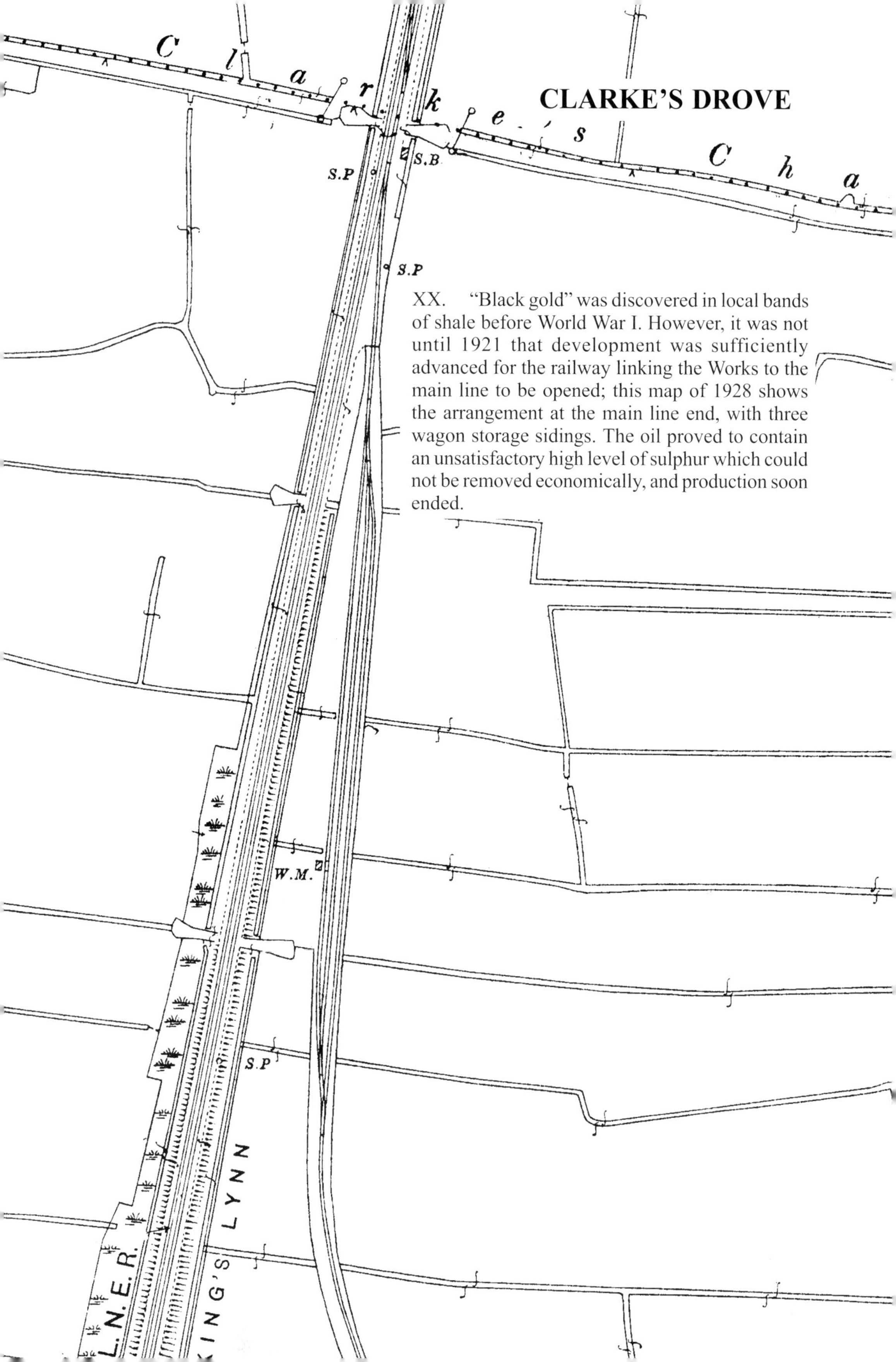

XX. "Black gold" was discovered in local bands of shale before World War I. However, it was not until 1921 that development was sufficiently advanced for the railway linking the Works to the main line to be opened; this map of 1928 shows the arrangement at the main line end, with three wagon storage sidings. The oil proved to contain an unsatisfactory high level of sulphur which could not be removed economically, and production soon ended.

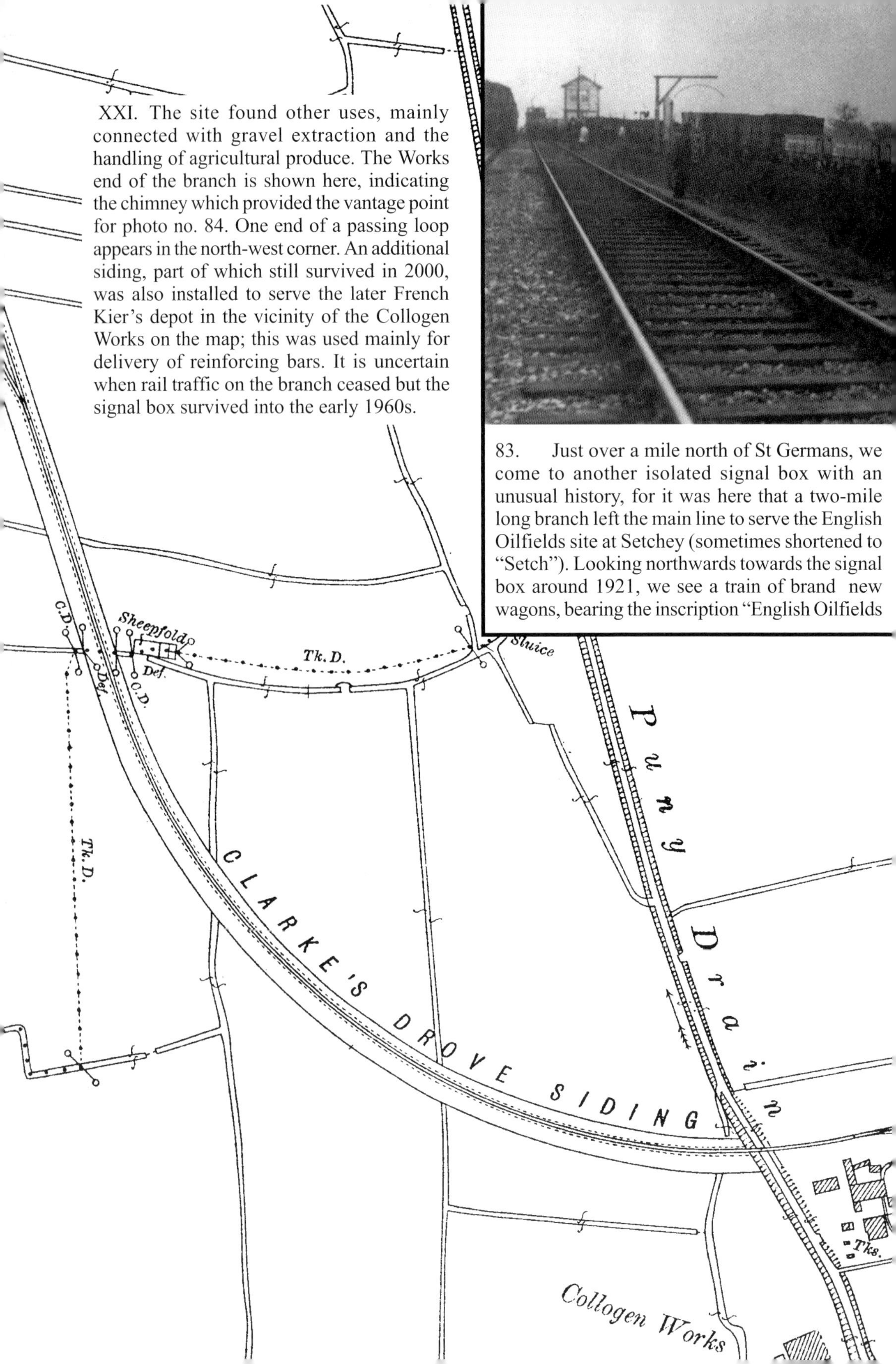

XXI. The site found other uses, mainly connected with gravel extraction and the handling of agricultural produce. The Works end of the branch is shown here, indicating the chimney which provided the vantage point for photo no. 84. One end of a passing loop appears in the north-west corner. An additional siding, part of which still survived in 2000, was also installed to serve the later French Kier's depot in the vicinity of the Collogen Works on the map; this was used mainly for delivery of reinforcing bars. It is uncertain when rail traffic on the branch ceased but the signal box survived into the early 1960s.

83. Just over a mile north of St Germans, we come to another isolated signal box with an unusual history, for it was here that a two-mile long branch left the main line to serve the English Oilfields site at Setchey (sometimes shortened to "Setch"). Looking northwards towards the signal box around 1921, we see a train of brand new wagons, bearing the inscription "English Oilfields

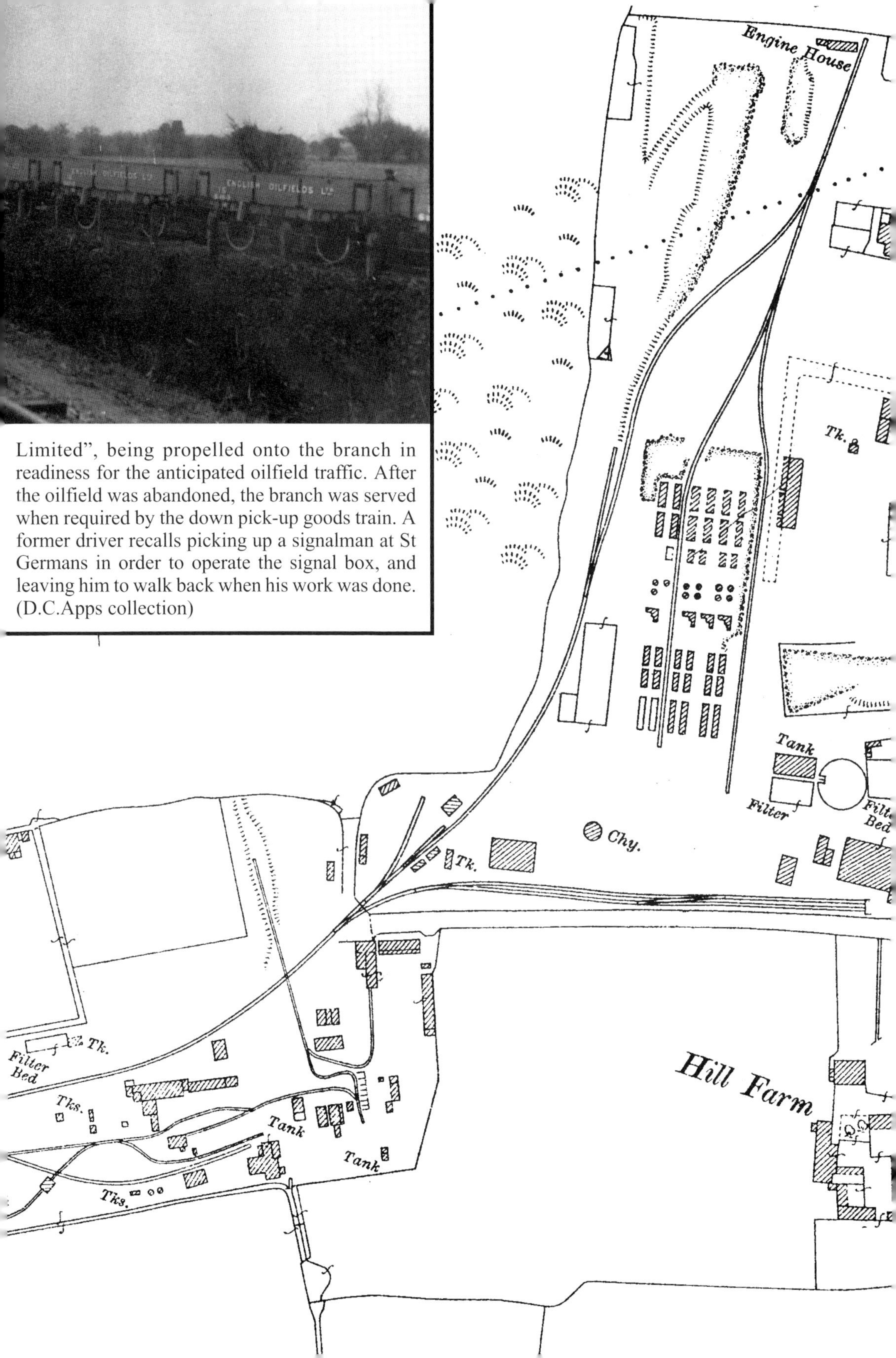

Limited", being propelled onto the branch in readiness for the anticipated oilfield traffic. After the oilfield was abandoned, the branch was served when required by the down pick-up goods train. A former driver recalls picking up a signalman at St Germans in order to operate the signal box, and leaving him to walk back when his work was done. (D.C.Apps collection)

84. This panorama northwards from the top of the 160 feet high chimney at the site gives an idea of the extent of the workings around 1920, with the main A10 road passing close to the huts on the right. A row of wagons stands on the rail track to the left, and some of these appear to be the 3-plank private owners we saw being delivered at Clarke's Drove. Beyond them, a siding terminates in the engine shed. English Oilfields Limited was the most successful – or least unsuccessful - of several companies formed to tap the oil deposits hereabouts, but production ceased in the 1930s and the company did not pay a dividend until the site was sold for redevelopment around 1961. Nearby Downham Market therefore remained a small country town, and was fated never to become the Dallas of West Norfolk. (D.C.Apps collection)

85. For a few years in the early 1920s the engine shed on the site was the home of a fireless locomotive, built by Andrew Barclay in 1917. Little is known of the earlier and later movements of this engine, but the initials D.E.S. on the running plate and boiler perhaps provide a clue to the previous owner. The four stalwarts of the workforce were obviously the subject of the photograph; nonetheless it provides us with a valuable glimpse of this unusual locomotive as it went about its work, well away from the public eye. (D.C.Apps collection)

86. For a while the oilfield was of sufficient importance to warrant a bus service from Kings Lynn, as the destination board proves. The crew of a solid tyred AEC product, operated by United Automobile Services, pose in front of their vehicle, which appears to have been built on a lorry chassis. The middle of the three gentlemen is probably the driver, whose overcoat would have been invaluable in the absence of a windscreen, whilst to his left is a youthful looking conductor with his cash bag. (D.C.Apps collection)

XXII. This map at the scale of 6 inches to 1 mile shows the relative position of the various railway locations on the southern approaches to the town as they existed in 1938. The Ely to Kings Lynn line and Kings Lynn Harbour Branch are clearly indicated. The connection to the former M&GN station at South Lynn is in the south-west corner while the branches from Dereham and Hunstanton meet the main line in the north-east corner.

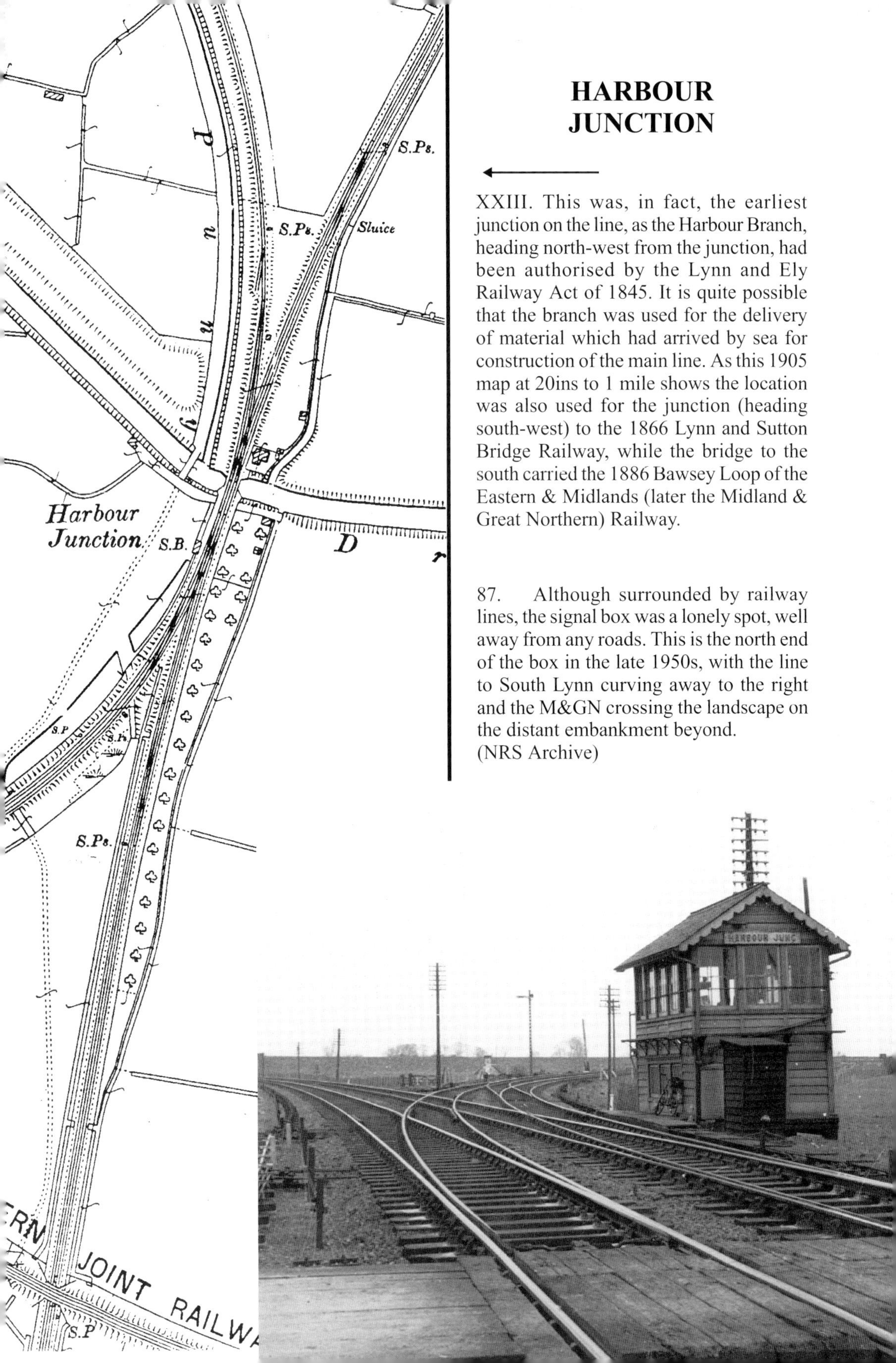

HARBOUR JUNCTION

←

XXIII. This was, in fact, the earliest junction on the line, as the Harbour Branch, heading north-west from the junction, had been authorised by the Lynn and Ely Railway Act of 1845. It is quite possible that the branch was used for the delivery of material which had arrived by sea for construction of the main line. As this 1905 map at 20ins to 1 mile shows the location was also used for the junction (heading south-west) to the 1866 Lynn and Sutton Bridge Railway, while the bridge to the south carried the 1886 Bawsey Loop of the Eastern & Midlands (later the Midland & Great Northern) Railway.

87. Although surrounded by railway lines, the signal box was a lonely spot, well away from any roads. This is the north end of the box in the late 1950s, with the line to South Lynn curving away to the right and the M&GN crossing the landscape on the distant embankment beyond. (NRS Archive)

88 . The photographer was having a "last day" trip over the former M&GN line on 28th February 1959, when he recorded the line from Ely curving gently round towards Harbour Junction, where it meets the connecting line from South Lynn. The large building on the skyline on the left belongs to West Norfolk Fertilisers, and a line of vans can be seen in its sidings, which from the late 1890s onwards were served by both the GER Harbour Branch and by the M&GN. (A.E.Bennett)

89. In later years, the peace of the place was shattered when Kings Lynn gained a much needed road bypass. The concrete span of the bypass bridge dominates the signalman's view northwards; beyond it, the Harbour Branch leaves the main line on the left and Campbell's siding diverges to the right. This picture dates from 9th October 1984, just a few days before the signal box was closed.
(R.J.Adderson)

90. Class 37 diesels dominated the passenger services for much of the diesel era. Seen from the bypass bridge, no. 37089 approaches the junction on 4th July 1981 with the 12.36 train from Liverpool Street, due in Kings Lynn at 14.42. In the centre of the picture, there is a gap in the former M&GN embankment where the bridge has been removed. (R.J.Adderson)

91. Campbells Soups opened their Kings Lynn factory in the Summer of 1959, and for the next thirty years or so made intensive use of rail transport from the network of sidings at the site. At the busiest times, up to fifteen loaded wagons left here each day, mostly for destinations in Scotland. Here we have a scene from the mid-1960s, as the white-coated General Manager of the factory, and two other employees watch the loading of a pallet load of assorted canned soup onto a waiting van. In later years, curtain sided wagons in "Campbells" livery provided distinctive transport for the outgoing cans, but the traffic was lost to road transport following the withdrawal of the Speedlink freight service in the early 1990s. Soon afterwards the tracks from the sidings were lifted and found further use on the North Norfolk Railway. (Courtesy Campbells Grocery Products Ltd)

4. Kings Lynn Harbour Branc

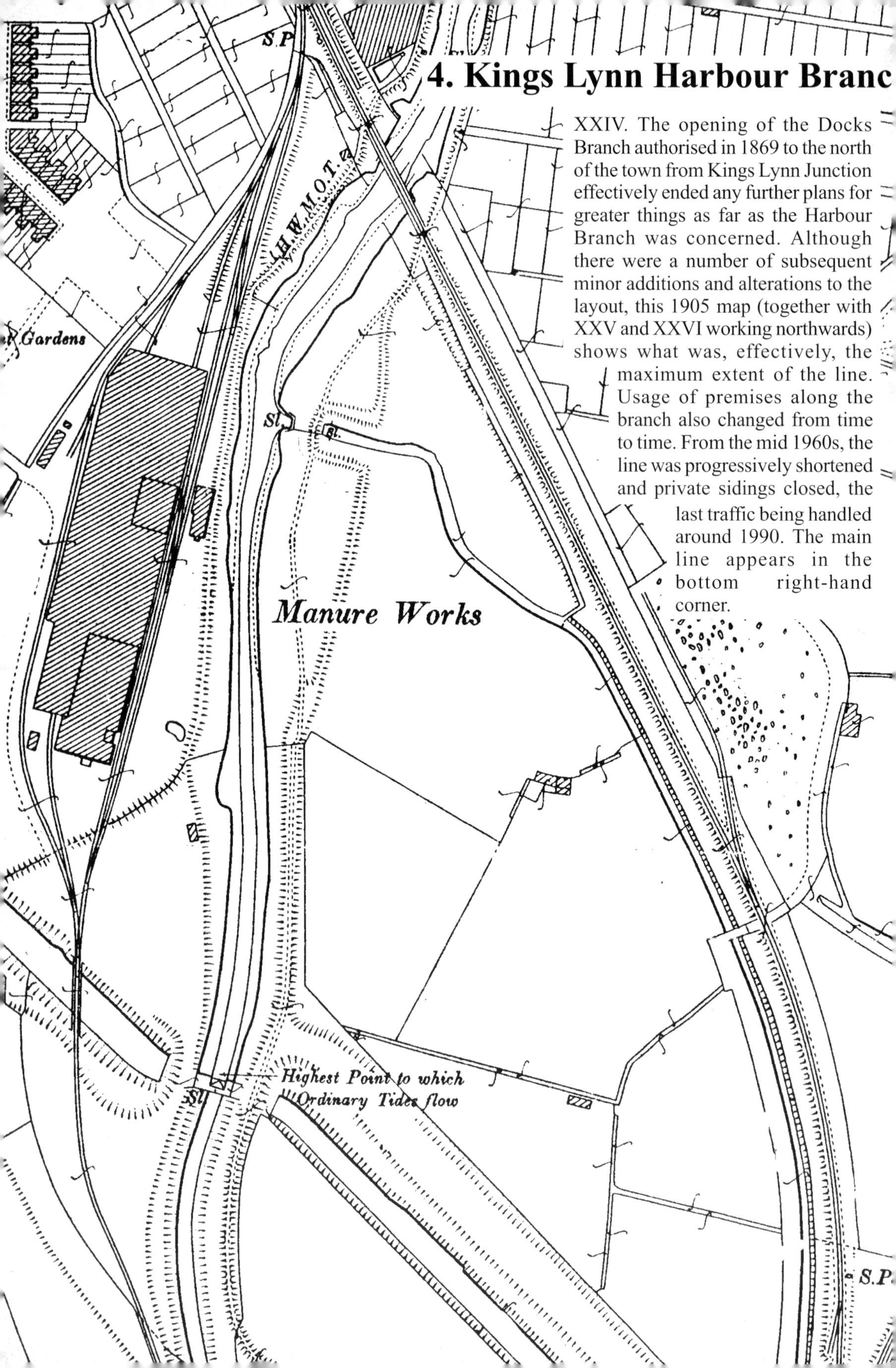

XXIV. The opening of the Docks Branch authorised in 1869 to the north of the town from Kings Lynn Junction effectively ended any further plans for greater things as far as the Harbour Branch was concerned. Although there were a number of subsequent minor additions and alterations to the layout, this 1905 map (together with XXV and XXVI working northwards) shows what was, effectively, the maximum extent of the line. Usage of premises along the branch also changed from time to time. From the mid 1960s, the line was progressively shortened and private sidings closed, the last traffic being handled around 1990. The main line appears in the bottom right-hand corner.

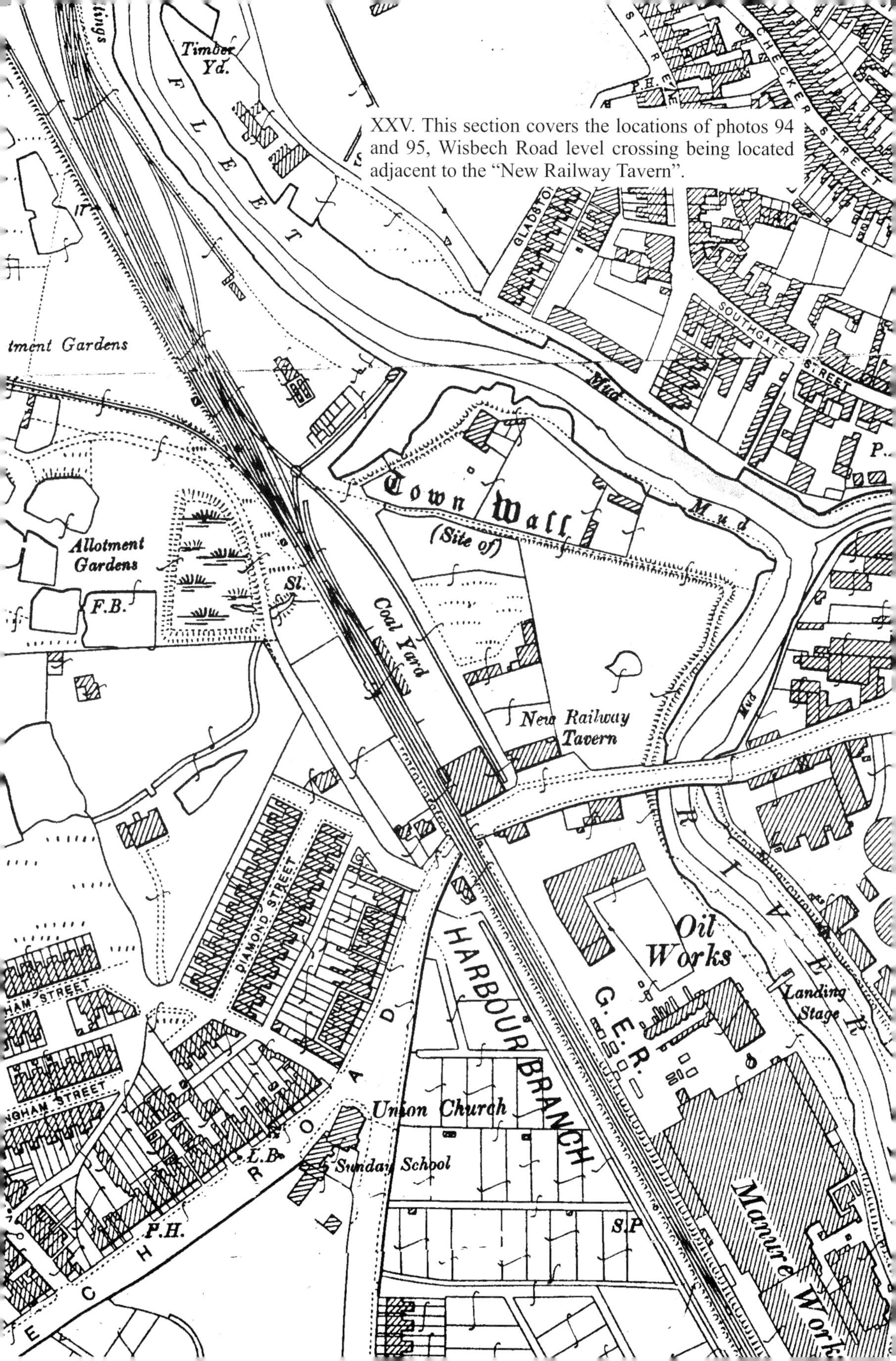

XXV. This section covers the locations of photos 94 and 95, Wisbech Road level crossing being located adjacent to the "New Railway Tavern".

XXVI. This section was, by far, the most complicated section of the branch, seeking to serve as many commercial premises as possible, despite the constraints of the site. The branch terminated a short distance beyond the northern edge of the map adjacent to the Purfleet.

92. Typifying the final form of freight traffic on the branch, no. 08713 brings four grain wagons towards the junction on 9th October 1984. The shunter will take its train round the curve to South Lynn, and run round there before hauling the wagons back to Kings Lynn yard. (R.J.Adderson)

93. Deep within the West Norfolk Fertilisers complex we see one of the wagon tipplers in operation – by 1951 four such tipplers were available to simplify the discharge of bulk raw materials. Established in 1872, the Company was taken over by Fisons in 1965, but production at the 50-acre site ceased two years later. (R.Goodchild)

94. The distinctive West Norfolk Fertilisers building features again in this picture looking towards the junction from Wisbech Road level crossing around 1960. On the left a line of wagons occupies the private siding which kept this section of line in use until the 1980s. (NRS Archive)

95. North of the crossing, the branch was operated as a goods yard, serving several industrial premises as well as the harbour itself. The scotch padlocked to the rails marks the furthest extent of the signalman's jurisdiction, and all train movements beyond this point were the responsibility of staff in the yard. (NRS Archive)

96. A shirt sleeved official checks the progress of rebuilding work on Boal Quay on 7th May 1952. There are plenty of railway wagons in the sidings by the Harbour Branch on the far side of the Nar, which flows into the Ouse behind the crane at the south end of the Quay. (R.Goodchild)

97. As well as bringing the map to life, the panorama northwards from a similar elevated viewpoint a few months later shows that some of the construction materials have arrived by rail on the bogie bolster wagon. The River Nar swing bridge is to the right of the picture, and the East Coast Shipping Co. premises are below the chimney in the centre - the adjacent Mill Fleet bridge is obscured by the wagons on the quayside. (R.Goodchild)

98. The swing bridge over the River Nar dated from 1854, and was still in working order when photographed on 2nd February 1966. However, the warning sign, a century or so younger, is not wearing so well. (J.Watling)

99. A tractor was photographed on the same day, propelling two wagons over the bridge, with the cranes on Boal Quay beyond. At this time the tractor was kept in the converted railway stables, providing a link with the previous mode of shunting at this end of the line. (J.Watling)

100. The winding equipment of the bridge was delightfully unsophisticated, with a large handle operating the geared mechanism. On the far side of the structure, to the left of the handle, the builders plate reveals that the bridge had been constructed by H & M D Grissell, of Regents Canal Ironworks in London. (J.Watling)

101. Another swing bridge, this one dating back to 1855, carried the single track over the muddy waters of the Mill Fleet. Both bridges were demolished in early 1970, some eighteen months after rail traffic ceased on this northern section of the branch. (R.F.Bonny)

102. Beyond the Mill Fleet bridge, the lines continued along South Quay for another quarter of a mile or so. A lorry, whose load is being transferred to the coaster *Nottingham*, blocks the tracks, which are set into the cobbles on the quayside. The loading gantry links this picture with the previous one. (R.Barham collection)

5. Harbour Junction to Kings Lynn

NORTH OF HARBOUR JUNCTION

103.Class D16/3 4-4-0 no. 2614 heads "The Fenman" express south of Kings Lynn. The 6.45 a.m. from Hunstanton to Liverpool Street and 4.30 p.m. in the reverse direction acquired "The Fenman" title in 1949, and this photograph must have been taken in its very early days, for the locomotive still carries its LNER number and livery. (Alan M. Wells collection, M&GN Circle)

EXTONS ROAD AND KINGS LYNN JUNCTION

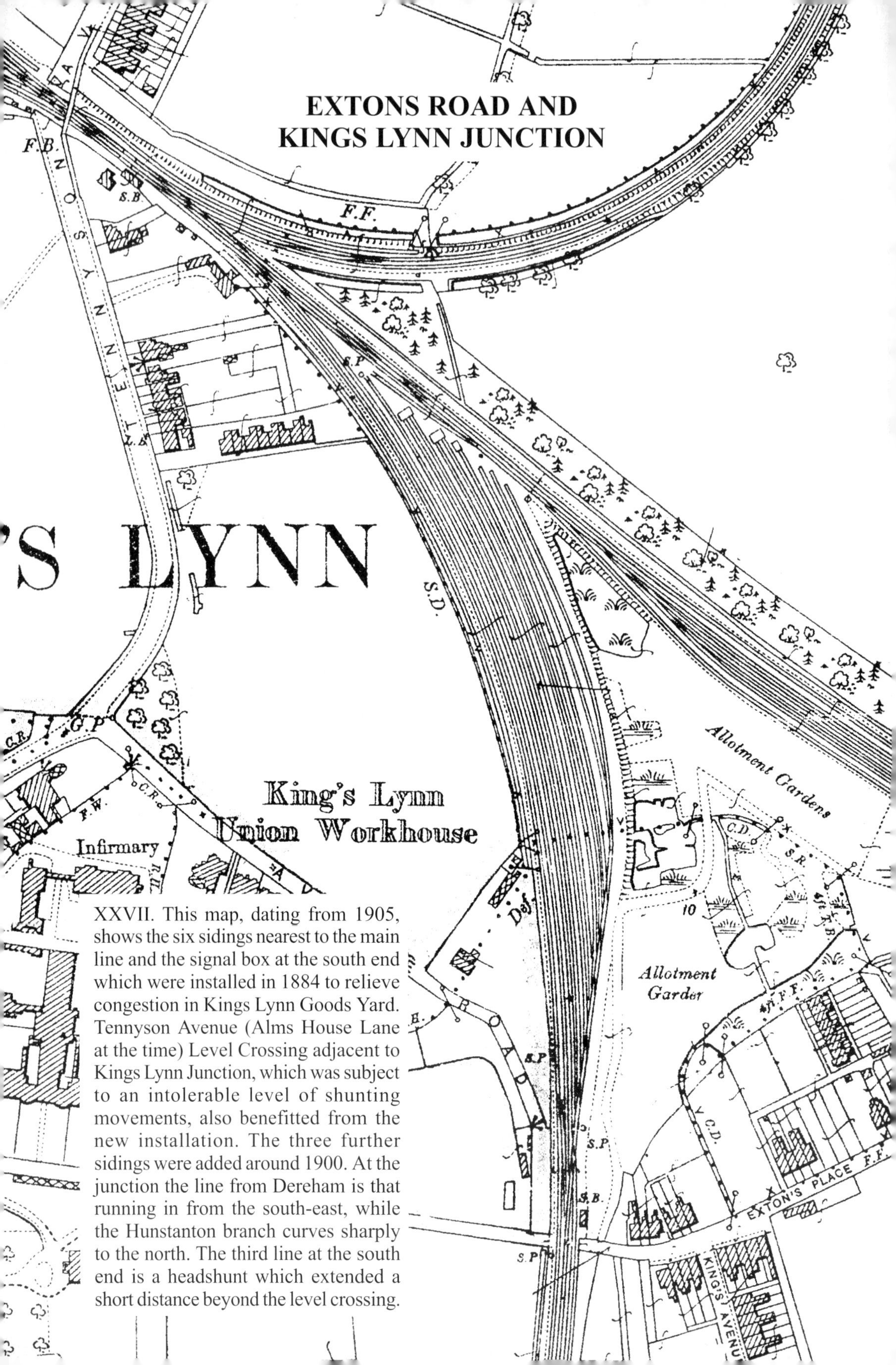

XXVII. This map, dating from 1905, shows the six sidings nearest to the main line and the signal box at the south end which were installed in 1884 to relieve congestion in Kings Lynn Goods Yard. Tennyson Avenue (Alms House Lane at the time) Level Crossing adjacent to Kings Lynn Junction, which was subject to an intolerable level of shunting movements, also benefitted from the new installation. The three further sidings were added around 1900. At the junction the line from Dereham is that running in from the south-east, while the Hunstanton branch curves sharply to the north. The third line at the south end is a headshunt which extended a short distance beyond the level crossing.

104. Looking along the sidings from the north in Great Eastern days, we see an 0-6-0 tank engine at the head of a long goods train. At least half of the vehicles are cattle wagons, showing visible evidence of the lime washing used for hygienic purposes on such trains. The signal box, which was replaced by a ground frame in 1940, is out of sight round the curve, whilst the Dereham line comes in past the somewhat unsteady looking signal on the left. Usage of the sidings declined from the late 1960s onwards, and the last rusting tracks were removed in the mid 1980s. (National Railway Museum)

105. Until it was demolished in 1991, the footbridge over Tennyson Avenue provided a grandstand view of the approaches to Kings Lynn station. From this viewpoint, the spectator could see the line from Ely curving in from the right to join the line from Dereham, with wagons stabled in Extons Road sidings in the angle of the junction. The lines to the left bear off northwards to Hunstanton. This picture dates from around 1960; the signal box survived to control train movements, albeit over a much reduced track layout, into the 21st century. (NRS Archive)

106. The opposite side of the bridge provided an equally comprehensive view towards the station. Providing a connection with the M&GN route, Class N7 0-6-2T no.69698 propels a train for South Lynn towards the junction on 25th September 1958. With up to twenty return trips a day on a journey of fractionally over two miles, this service was ideally suited to pull-push working. It also added considerably to the volume of traffic between the station and Harbour Junction. The branch line to the docks curves away in a north-westerly direction beyond the fine signal gantry controlling departures from the goods yard to the south, east and north. (B. Harrison)

107. As no. 47583 *County of Hertfordshire* sets out with the 09.05 for London on 9th October 1984, the goods yard is a hive of activity. Trains of limestone from Wirksworth and oil from Shellhaven, both bound for South Lynn beet factory, occupy the arrival lines, whilst in the distance another class 47 waits to leave with the sand train from Middleton Towers. A pair of class 20 diesels stands on the right, ready to take the limestone empties back to Derbyshire. (R.J.Adderson)

108. Remaining on the footbridge, we see a J69 0-6-0T and a D16/3 4-4-0 simmering outside the shed on 31st March 1955. Above the Gresley coaches, another distinctive signal gantry controls the lines from the passenger station. The poster boards, nondescript huts, battered oil drums, and even the attempts at cultivation in the bottom left hand corner combine with the more obvious railway features to produce a picture oozing with atmosphere. (J.H.Meredith)

109. Nearly 35 years later, the same fencing provides the foreground to a very different scene. On a November afternoon in 1989 the last rays of the Winter sun illuminate a Network SouthEast DMU as it sets out for Cambridge on the single track, passing between the empty goods yard and the deserted diesel shed and fuelling facilities. (R.J.Adderson)

110. A "Sandringham" class 4-6-0 is about to pass under the footbridge one day in the late 1950s, with a train whose coaches suggest a through working between the Midlands and Hunstanton. Next to the upturned fogman's hut in the foreground, a set of miniature signals repeats the arrangement of the gantry seen in picture 108. (H.N.James/J.Day)

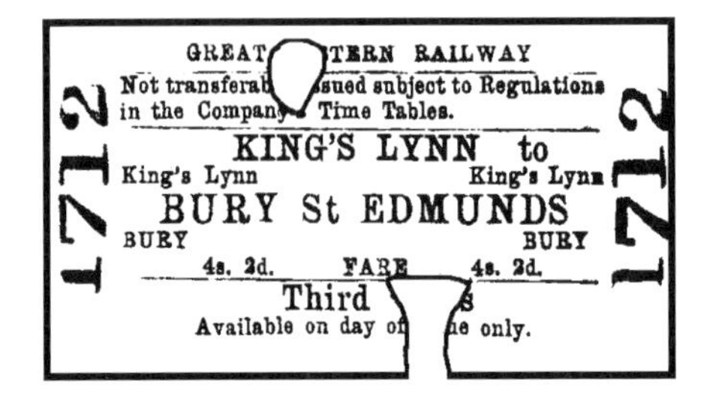

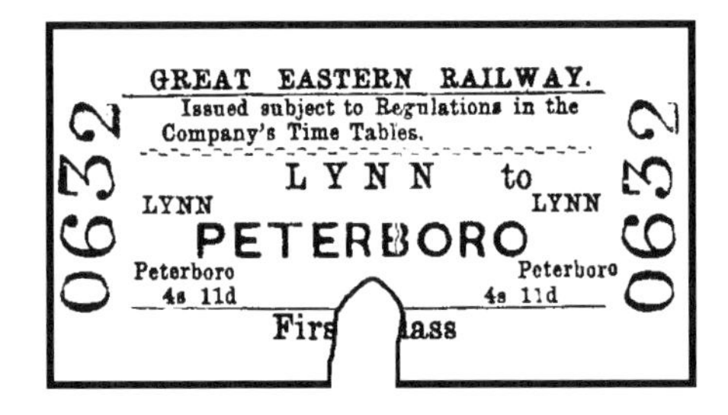

KINGS LYNN

111. Here we see the approach to the station in GER days. The shed on the extreme left, dating from 1903/4, is used to stable the royal train, whilst the three-plank structure guarded by an ornate lamp standard is the ticket platform. Passengers arriving after a long journey must have been extremely frustrated by the stop here, within sight of the station platforms, while their tickets were inspected. Five wagons loaded with locomotive coal stand in the siding to the right. (National Railway Museum)

112. The water tower and shed offices are prominent in this picture looking in the opposite direction around 1900. A class T19 2-4-0 is making use of the turntable, and we have a further glimpse of the ticket platform on the extreme right. (HMRS, Hilton Collection)

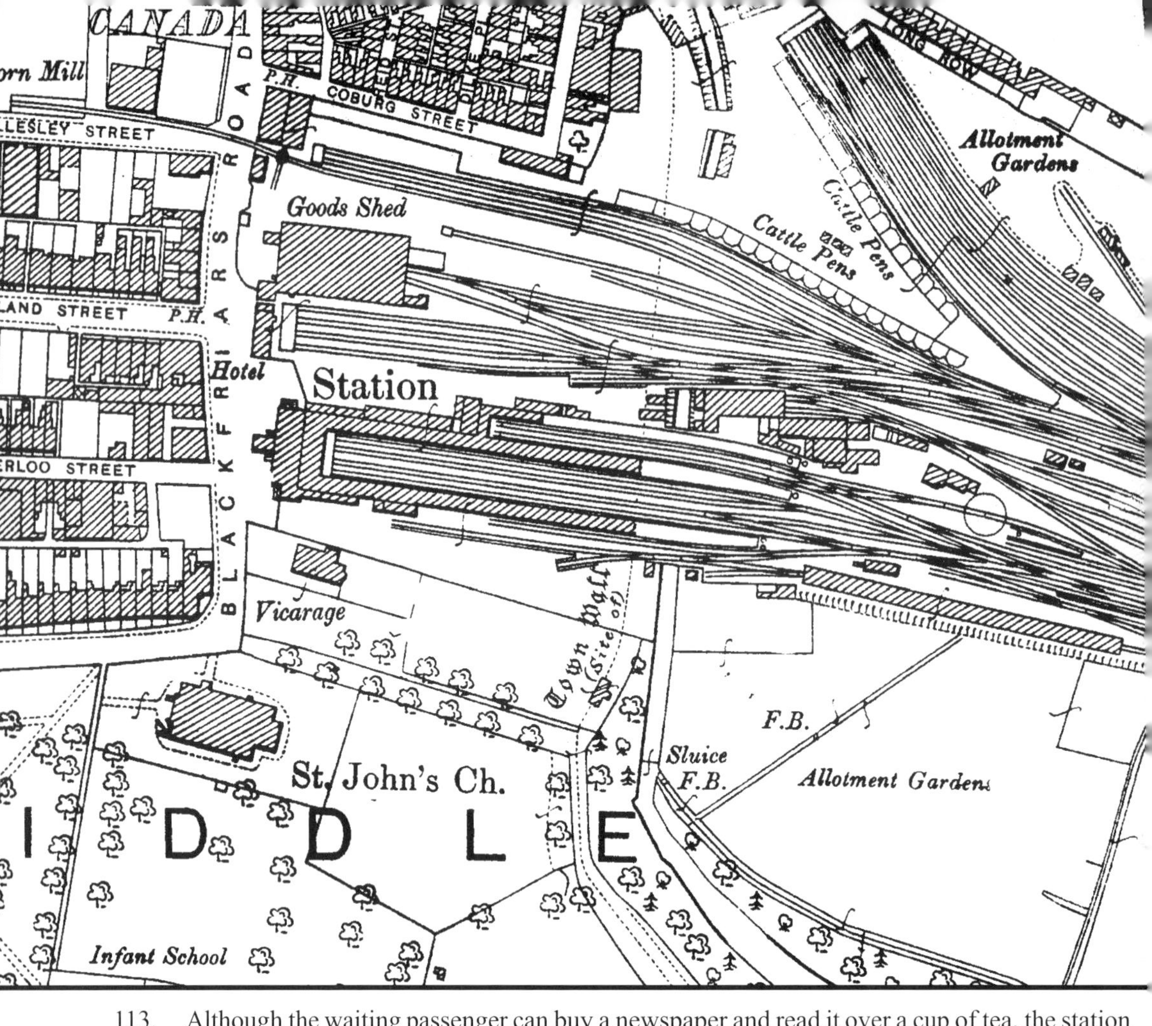

113. Although the waiting passenger can buy a newspaper and read it over a cup of tea, the station concourse appears cramped and dingy. Behind the front wheel of the bicycle, a flysheet reference to "The Crisis" suggests Munich and a 1938 dateline. This area was smartened up considerably in later years, but the refreshment room remained in the same location. (Stations UK)

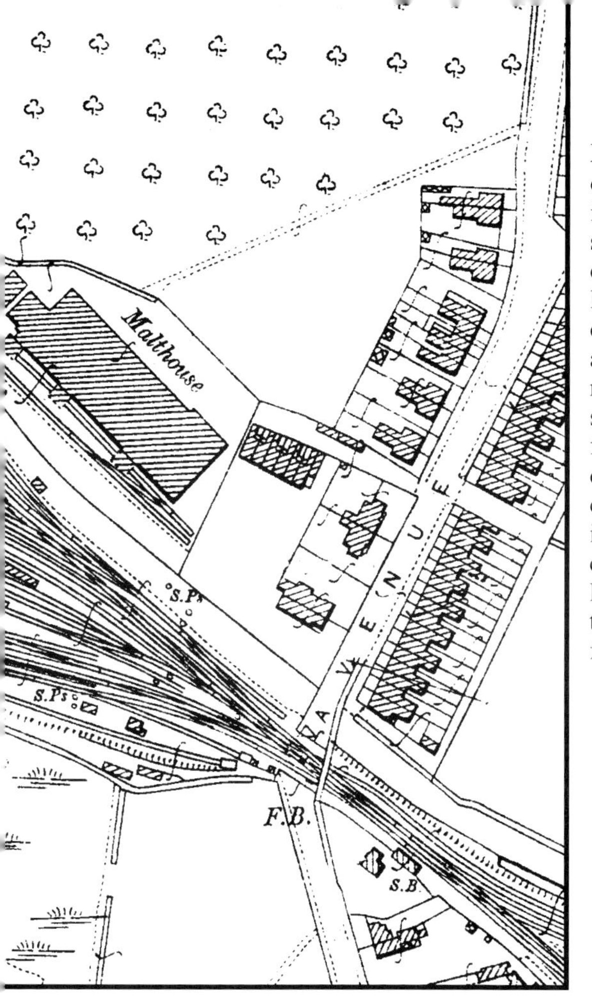

XXVIII. For completeness, this map overlaps that for Kings Lynn Junction and is of the same date. The original passenger station was located on the site of the goods depot, but, unlike the other stations on the line, which were all built using the local carstone, it was of timber construction and a fairly rudimentary affair, despite its overall roof. It was replaced in 1871 on the present site, allowing the goods yard, and other facilities, space to expand. This they did down the years, but the site always appeared cramped, mainly due to the presence of the increasingly busy Tennyson Avenue level crossing at the eastern approaches. The Docks Branch veers to the north towards the top of the map past the malthouse; this will feature in a later volume.

114. Opened on 28th August 1871, the replacement station building has changed only in detail over the years. When this picture was taken in the 1950s, the awning over the steps had been cut back from a previous elaborate form, and this, in turn, was replaced by a plainer construction by the early 1960s. (J.Watling collection)

115. With five main traffic flows – to Dereham, Hunstanton, March, Ely and the M&GN – the station could be a very busy place. At least three of the five platforms, as well as the centre roads, are occupied on 21st May 1957. Class D16/3 4-4-0 no. 62592 leaves platform 1 past the signal box, a sister loco is signalled out of platform 3, and two Ivatt 4MT 2-6-0s from the ex-M&GN line are adding their contributions to the generally smoky atmosphere. (R.C.Riley)

116. The GER "Claud Hamilton" 4-4-0s in their original and rebuilt forms were a familiar sight here for over fifty years. By 14th February 1959, no. 62606 has survived long enough to share the platforms with one of its diesel successors, Brush Type 2 no. D5507. (A.E.Bennett)

117. The network of sidings, yards and goods branches meant that Kings Lynn was always well endowed with shunting locos. Towards the end of the steam era, two class J69 0-6-0Ts, nos 68542 and 68499, pause between duties near the site of the original terminus on 14th February 1959. (A.E.Bennett)

118. Members of the Royal family were regular visitors to Lynn on their journeys to and from Sandringham. Sometimes they travelled through to Wolferton station on the Hunstanton line; sometimes road transport was provided for the last leg of the journey. The special train headcode together with the painted tyres, buffers and pipework reveal that D5553 and a sister loco are on Royal Train duty early in 1967. In January 1961 a loco of this class had failed with a down train conveying royalty, and the passengers arrived 57 minutes late after being rescued by a B1 from Cambridge. As a result, the return working was provided with a "Britannia", and for many years afterwards the embarrassed authorities were reluctant to entrust Royal workings to a single Brush Type 2! (R.F.Bonny)

119. The station was refurbished prior to electrification, and the extended platform and modern lighting are prominent here. No.317354 is the nearest of the three Class 317 EMUs stabled for the weekend on 1st February 1997. These units monopolised the services prior to the introduction of the Class 365s, and quickly established a reputation for reliability, even if they were not as comfortable as the previous rakes of loco-hauled coaches. (R.J.Adderson)

120. A last look back along the platform shows no. 70000 *Britannia* standing at the buffers with a night-time arrival. This "steam-age" picture was taken as recently as October 1991, when the Pacific worked a number of special trains to and from Ely. Nearly forty years earlier, on 11th February 1952, this engine had worked the funeral train for King George VI between Kings Lynn and London. (D.C.Pearce)